Pictorial BIBLE ATLAS

J. Catling Allen

CWR

THE Bible is the world's most treasured religious book. It is read by millions of people all over the world – not only by Jews and Christians, but also by people of other religions, for although it was written so long ago, its message is timeless. Christians believe that God continues to speak to us today through the Bible, revealing the truth about Himself and the way we should live. This is why Christians often call the Bible the written Word of God, and believe that God guided and helped the writers to record His message to mankind. Christians therefore call the Bible an 'inspired' book, believing that it has divine authority.

But the religious message of the Bible cannot be truly understood without some knowledge of its geographical and historical background. The purpose of this Bible atlas, therefore, is to help students understand the Bible better by providing a series of simple maps, accompanying texts and photographs to illustrate the geographical and historical setting of the Bible story.

The text relates the maps to the relevant events recorded in the Bible and places them in their geographical and historical setting. Recent archaeological discoveries are also mentioned in view of their importance to biblical studies, and Bible references are given where appropriate.

The atlas begins with an introductory section on the Bible and Bible Lands and a bird's-eye view of the Bible. This is followed by two main sections covering the Old and New Testament periods – summarised by time charts – and a short section of two maps showing the spread of Christianity. Finally, there is a section on Archaeology and the Bible concluding with two maps showing important archaeological sites in Bible Lands.

Copyright © 1980, 2009, John Catling Allen

First published as *Pictorial Bible Atlas* 1980, 1982, by Hulton Educational Publications Ltd.

This edition published 2009 by CWR, Waverley Abbey House, Waverley Lane, Farnham, Surrey GU9 8EP, UK.
Registered Charity No. 294387. Registered Limited Company No. 1990308.

The right of John Catling Allen to be identified as the author of this work has been asserted by him in accordance with the Copyright, Designs and Patents Act 1988.

Unless otherwise indicated, all Scripture references are from the Holy Bible: New International Version (NIV), copyright © 1973, 1978, 1984 by the International Bible Society.

Birds-eye View of the Bible based on the teachings of Philip Greenslade.

Editing, design and production by CWR

Printed in China by C&C Offset Printing

ISBN: 978-1-85345-534-6

Acknowledgements

THE author is grateful for the helpful advice and comments on this book received from Miss Elizabeth Moore and Mr Stephen Thompson.

All photos including cover taken by the author.

John Catling Allen

JOHN Catling Allen was an Anglican parish priest until retirement. He is the author of other educational books, including *The Journeys of St Paul*, and he has conducted countless tours, particularly in the Near and Middle East. As a result, he built up the J Catling Allen photo library and, for many years, was a Swan Hellenic guest lecturer.

Shrine at Wadi Musa, built over the Fountain of Moses

Contents

Model of Herod's Temple, Jerusalem

THE *Cover to Cover Bible Atlas* takes you on a tour of the Bible's events in their geographical setting through topographical maps and shows you some of its archaeology through full-colour photographs. Accompanying the maps and pictures is a summary of biblical history in chronological order, from the life of Abraham through to the churches of Revelation.

The Bible is the true story of all that exists, from first creation to new creation. It shows us who God is, what He likes and dislikes, what He thinks and feels, and what He plans and does, by telling how He interacts with people and events in the past, the present and the future.

And our lives – our personal stories – are redeemed from insignificance and futility by being reattached to God's big story and His strategic plan for the renewal of the world and the implementation of His permanent reign of justice, peace and joy.

The biblical story is an enthralling, but long and complicated, epic with numerous twists, turns and sub-plots. This bird's-eye view of its main 'plot line' should help you to see the big picture and keep the sub-plots – many of the Bible stories you already know – in the context of God's overall redemptive plan and action. All smaller stories gain significance through being in connection with – and sometimes in tension with – the overarching narrative or 'plot line' of biblical history.

Jesus is the hub and the climax of that history. Without the Old Testament we cannot really understand Jesus. We need the entire Old Testament story in order to clearly see who Jesus is.

At the heart of the Bible's epic story are five major covenants – solemn pledges, usually sealed in blood (death) – by which God expresses His loving commitment to save the world He has made. They are called the 'covenants of promise' in Ephesians 2:12, and they are referred to over forty times in the New Testament simply as the 'promise' (eg Acts 26:6). These covenants are part of the Bible's five main stories which help us to grasp and interpret the Bible's 'plot':

1. **The Flood story:** *the Noahic Covenant* preserves the earth for God's future redemption.
2. **The story of Abraham:** *the Abrahamic Covenant* sets in motion the promise-plan of God by guaranteeing a people, located at the crossroads of the world, through whom God will bless all nations.
3. **The Exodus from Egypt:** *the Mosaic Covenant* creates God's covenant 'son' Israel, to enlighten the world.
4. **The Kingdom established:** *the Davidic Covenant* guarantees a dynasty, a throne and a kingdom that will last forever (called a covenant in Psalm 89:3–4).
5. **The story of Jesus:** *the New Covenant* brings God's promise-plan to fulfilment.

These five covenant stories carry the main narrative forward to its intended conclusion. There is a cumulative effect as each of these major stories gathers up and enlarges upon earlier ones, and every covenantal connection eventually leads to Jesus. The first four 'covenants of promise' point the way to – and climax in – Jesus the Messiah (King) and His New Covenant which fulfils the promises and expectations of the previous four covenants. It also becomes the launch pad for worldwide blessing and the eventual renewal of creation, the final kingdom (reign) of God.

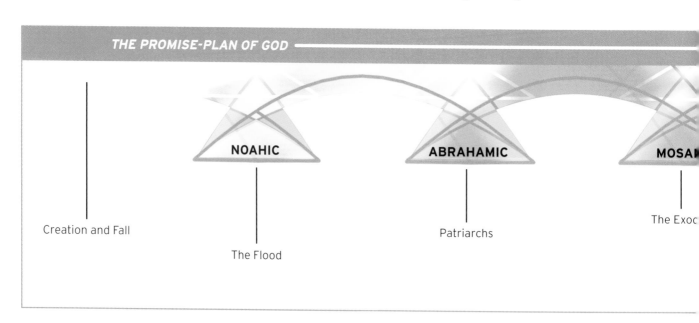

THE PROMISE-PLAN OF GOD

NOAHIC   ABRAHAMIC   MOSA[...]

Creation and Fall   Patriarchs   The Exo[...]

The Flood

Where the action is

The events of the Old Testament can be summarised as the birth, death and resurrection of Israel, the people of God. Israel develops from being a family, to a tribe, to a people (in Egypt) to a nation (under Moses), and finally to being a kingdom (under David). God's unfolding plan and covenantal promises then narrow to concentrate in the person of the king and the capital city of Jerusalem, where God's Temple was located.

The kings of Israel (and their subjects) repeatedly broke God's covenant, and eventually God punished the nation – first with the splitting of the kingdom into two kingdoms, then the destruction of both kingdoms, culminating in deportation (exile) to a foreign land (2 Chronicles 36:14–21).

Some Jews eventually returned to Jerusalem and rebuilt the Temple, but the Jews never saw the Davidic kingdom restored. Thus the condition of 'exile' persisted long after the return to the promised land, and at the time of Christ (Messiah), the Jews were still exiles, 'sheep without a shepherd', awaiting a new king and a new covenant.

That previous national history was re-enacted by the Messiah who is both a new Moses and a new David. As God's Son-King, He redefines Israel, expounds the *spirit* of Israel's Law, rescinds its dietary restrictions (Mark 7:19) and expands the boundaries of the covenant to include the marginalised and (eventually) Gentiles. He also gathers Israel around Himself, appointing twelve new leaders (His apostles), and He reconstitutes Israel in Himself.

In a startling reversal of the usual covenantal arrangements, the covenant *maker* (God, in Christ) dies for the covenant *breaker* (Israel). Jesus' Messianic claims to son-kingship are vindicated through His resurrection (Romans 1:4). He then ascends to heaven where He is enthroned as King of all kings and Lord of all lords.

Jesus' New Covenant 'in His blood' is an individual covenant, not an ethnic or national one. It bestows on Jesus' loyal subjects forgiveness of sins, spiritual regeneration, eternal life and even *adoption*. It will ultimately lead to a whole new creation (Isaiah 65:17). It is sealed by the gift of the promised Holy Spirit (Acts 2:33; Ephesians 1:13) who restores the image of God in humankind, sharing with them God's own nature (2 Peter 1:4), empowering them to obey the royal law of love (James 2:8) and preparing them to reign with Messiah.

Forgiven and filled with God's Spirit, the members of the New Covenant community become participants in, and examples of, the coming new creation. They expand Messiah's realm by announcing the good news (1 Corinthians 15:3–8) as they await His return from heaven (1 Thessalonians 1:10) and the public revelation and manifestation of His kingdom (Revelation 1:7) which ultimately ushers in a whole new creation (Isaiah 65:17; Revelation 21:1–5) where humanity lives in the immediate presence of God.

The main events of this epic story fit into the covenantal scheme as illustrated below.

Come along now as we take you through the biblical story in a little more detail and show you the geographical 'stage' where the action takes place, along with some of the most important archaeological 'props'.

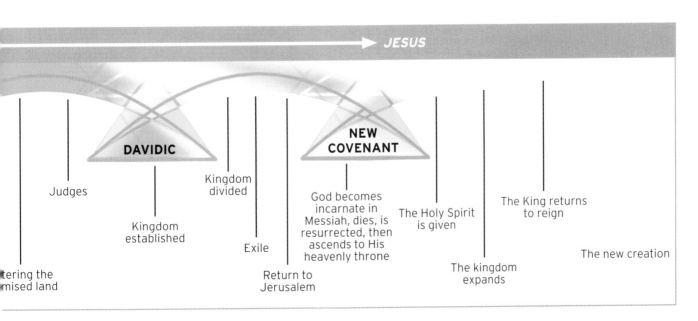

THE Bible is a collection of Jewish and Christian sacred writings, or holy Scriptures. So, strictly speaking, the Bible is not one book but a collection of books in one volume: in fact, the word 'Bible' comes from the Greek word '*biblia*' which means 'books'.

These books were written by many different authors in three different languages – Hebrew, Aramaic and Greek – at widely different times between around 950 BC and AD 100. The books are also very different, and contain a wide variety of literature: history, laws, poems and prayers, proverbs and prophecy, letters and sermons. But, in spite of their diversity, there is an underlying unity running through them. For they all reveal – directly or indirectly – the truth about God and His will for mankind. This is why they were collected and bound together under one cover to form the Book we now know as the Bible.

The complete Bible has sixty-six books which are divided into two sections – the Old Testament and the New Testament. The Old Testament has thirty-nine books. They are the sacred writings of the Jewish people, but Christians also accept them as

holy Scripture. They were originally written on scrolls, either in Hebrew or Aramaic, between the tenth and second centuries BC. Later, they were arranged in three groups: The Law, The Prophets and The Writings.

None of the original Old Testament manuscripts have survived and, until recently, the oldest manuscripts dated from the tenth century AD. But in 1947 the first Dead Sea Scrolls were discovered at Qumran. Among them were manuscripts of all the Old Testament books except Esther, dating from not later than the first century AD and the oldest manuscript (Isaiah) is dated from c.100 BC. Although they are some thousand years earlier than the tenth-century manuscripts, their texts are very similar.

The New Testament has twenty-seven books. They were written in Greek by Christians during the first and second centuries AD.

Like the books in the Old Testament, the New Testament books were only gradually collected together to form one volume. In fact, it was not until the fourth century AD that the list, or canon, of books to be included in the

New Testament was finally decided by the Church. The four Gospels telling the story of Jesus come first. They are followed by the Acts of the Apostles telling the story of the Early Church up to about AD 62. Then there are twenty-one letters written by the apostle Paul and other leading first-century Christians. Last of all is the Revelation, a book of visions about God's final victory over evil.

The exact dating of the New Testament books is uncertain, but biblical scholars think that Paul's early letters were the first to be written. They are dated between AD 48 and AD 60, that is, before the four Gospels and most of the other books, which are thought to have been written between AD 65 and AD 100.

Although none of the original New Testament manuscripts have survived there are many ancient Greek texts in existence. The earliest is a papyrus fragment of John's Gospel dating from around AD 125. Among the others is a fourth-century manuscript called the *Codex Sinaiticus* which contains the complete New Testament.

St Catherine's Monastery, Mount Sinai

Ancient Scroll of the Pentateuch

This ancient Codex, or manuscript, was discovered by chance in St Catherine's Monastery on Mount Sinai in 1844, and the principal surviving portion is now in the British Library.

By the middle of the third century the New Testament was being translated from early Greek manuscripts into other languages such as Syriac, Coptic and Latin. The first English translation was made in the fourteenth century when the complete Bible was translated into English for the first time. Known as 'Wycliffe's Bible', it was translated from a fourth-century Latin version called the Vulgate. After the invention of printing in the fifteenth century, further English translations were made, including the famous King James or Authorised Version of 1611, which has remained in use up to the present time. However, since the nineteenth century, many new English translations have been made based on the most accurate ancient texts and take into account the results of modern biblical scholarship.

ALTHOUGH the story of the Bible is centred on the small land of Israel/ Palestine, it cannot be understood without reference to the surrounding lands. For, owing to its geographical position, Palestine was greatly influenced in ancient times by the history and culture of the nations surrounding it. The biblical record of God's revelation, therefore, must be placed in the geographical, historical and cultural context in which it was written.

The importance of Palestine in the history of the ancient world lies in the fact that it is situated in the Fertile Crescent (see map on pages 10–11). This is the name given to the fertile area around the Arabian desert. It forms a semi-circle from Egypt up through Palestine and Syria, and then follows the Tigris and Euphrates down through Mesopotamia (the 'land between the rivers') to the Persian Gulf.

The Fertile Crescent was an early centre of civilisation because the waters of the rivers Tigris and Euphrates, the Jordan and the Nile made the land fertile. People naturally settled in these regions where there was plenty of water, rich soil and a hot climate, which enabled them to grow crops and keep animals. The eastern end of the Fertile Crescent is generally thought to have been one of the earliest centres of civilisation.

The Sumerians (a non-Semitic race who may have come from the east – Genesis 11:2) were the first known people to settle here, around 3500 BC. They founded a kingdom known as Sumer (biblical Shinar) which consisted of a number of city-states such as Uruk (biblical Erech), Ur and Eridu. The development of their civilisation and culture has been revealed by excavations on the sites of Sumerian cities in present-day Iraq. At Uruk, for example, archaeologists found hundreds of small clay tablets with a primitive form of picture writing dating from around 3100 BC, which later developed into wedge-shaped writing known as 'cuneiform'.

The Sumerians continued their settled life until Semitic tribes from the desert invaded the fertile lands north of Sumer and began to attack their cities. By about 2350 BC, Sargon I, one of their chieftains, had founded the small kingdom of Akkad and conquered Sumer. He was the first great leader of the Semitic race, and the founder of an empire which stretched from Mesopotamia to the Mediterranean.

Meanwhile, another Semitic empire had been established around 2400 BC, in the Fertile Crescent, covering the whole of Syria and Palestine. It was a powerful Canaanite empire, and its existence has only recently been discovered as a result of recent excavations at Ebla in northern Syria (see pages 60, 62). These excavations have also revealed that Sargon's grandson, Narum-Sin of Akkad, conquered Ebla and burnt the city, including the royal palace, around 2250 BC. However, the Akkadian empire founded by Sargon I was brought to an end when people called Gutians descended on the Fertile Crescent from the Zagros mountains around 2200 BC.

The Fertile Crescent was again invaded by Semitic tribes around 2000 BC. They were the Amorites of the Old Testament, who came from the Arabian desert and established kingdoms throughout Syria and Mesopotamia. One of them was the kingdom of Babylon whose most famous king was Hammurabi (eighteenth century BC). He is noted for his code of laws resembling the later laws of Moses, and was the builder of Babylon's first Ziggurat. This was almost certainly the background for the Tower of Babel story in Genesis 11:1–9. (Babel is the Hebrew for Babylon.) Hammurabi also brought the whole of Mesopotamia under his rule, and founded the Old Babylonian Empire. Among the cities he conquered was Mari, the magnificent capital of another Amorite Kingdom on the Euphrates. Excavations here have provided biblical scholars with

The River Nile at Aswan in Egypt

valuable new information about the possible historical background of the Hebrew Patriarchs.

During the period of the Patriarchs, Syria and Palestine are thought to have been controlled by Egypt, which had been a powerful kingdom for centuries. The Nile Valley is very fertile and people settled here in the earliest times. Then, around 3100 BC, the two kingdoms of Upper and Lower Egypt were united by a king called Menes.

Under later kings, called Pharaohs, the Egyptians developed one of the world's greatest ancient civilisations which lasted for over 3,000 years. As well as constructing dams and canals to control the Nile and irrigate the land, they built great cities and enormous temples. But their most spectacular constructions were the massive pyramids. These were built as tombs for the early Pharaohs during the period known as the Old Kingdom (around 2700–2200 BC).

It was later, during the Middle Kingdom (around 2100–1750 BC) that Egypt probably first controlled

Palestine and Syria. However, around 1750 BC Egypt itself was invaded and conquered by Semitic people from the east whom the Egyptians called the Hyksos, 'rulers of foreign lands'. They made their capital at Avaris (biblical Rameses) in the Nile Delta. This is one of the reasons many biblical scholars place the story of Joseph's rise to power in Egypt during the Hyksos period, for it is evident from the account in Genesis that the Egyptian capital at this time was in the Delta area (Genesis 46:28–47:26).

By about 1550 BC the Egyptians had managed to drive out the hated Hyksos. Egypt was then reunited under the Pharaohs of the New Kingdom (around 1550–1080 BC). During this time Egypt became a major world power, and its empire stretched from the Nile to the Euphrates.

Meanwhile, the people living in the mountainous regions to the north and east of the Fertile Crescent were forming powerful new kingdoms. They were non-Semitic Indo-Aryan races who also invaded the Fertile Crescent. Among them were the Hurrians (the Horites of the Old Testament), who founded the kingdom of Mitanni about 1500 BC in the northern part of the Fertile Crescent, and the Hittites from Asia Minor. They were in constant conflict with each other – and Egypt. This meant that Palestine, owing to its strategic importance, was a continual battleground even before the Israelite conquest.

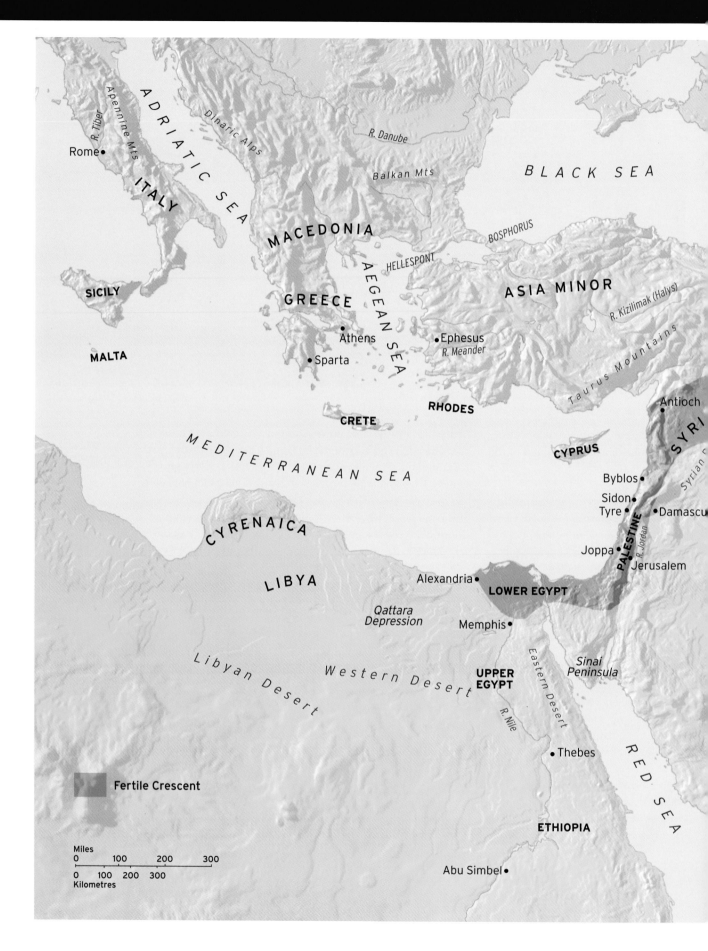

ADRIATIC SEA

ITALY

R. Tiber

Apennine Mts

Rome

SICILY

MALTA

Dinaric Alps

R. Danube

Balkan Mts

MACEDONIA

GREECE

Athens

Sparta

AEGEAN SEA

HELLESPONT

BOSPHORUS

BLACK SEA

ASIA MINOR

Ephesus
R. Meander

R. Kizilimak (Halys)

Taurus Mountains

RHODES

CRETE

MEDITERRANEAN SEA

CYPRUS

Antioch

SYRI

Syrian

Byblos

Sidon

Tyre

Joppa

PALESTINE

R. Jordan

Damascu

Jerusalem

CYRENAICA

LIBYA

Alexandria

*Qattara
Depression*

Memphis

LOWER EGYPT

Libyan Desert

Western Desert

UPPER
EGYPT

Eastern Desert

R. Nile

*Sinai
Peninsula*

RED SEA

Thebes

ETHIOPIA

Abu Simbel

Fertile Crescent

Miles
0   100   200   300

0   100   200   300
Kilometres

ARAL
SEA

R. Amu Darya (Oxus)

CASPIAN SEA

Caucasus Mountains

Kara Kum

ARMENIA

Elburz Mountains

• Nineveh

R. Tigris

• Ecbatana

Euphrates

MESOPOTAMIA

Zagros Mountains

IRAN
(PERSIA)

Babylon •

Ur •

• Persepolis

PERSIAN GULF

Arabian Desert

Rub al Khali

Ur. Excavation of a house associated with Abraham

Temple of Baal at Shechem

THE map overleaf shows the main journeys of the Hebrew Patriarchs – Abraham, Isaac and Jacob – as recorded in Genesis 11:31–46:27. These chapters tell us how God established a special relationship with these people and their descendants.

About the year 2000 BC God chose Abraham, 'a man of faith', to be the father and founder of the Hebrew race. The story begins when Terah, Abraham's father, migrated with his family from Ur in the Plain of Mesopotamia to Haran in the north. After Terah died God called Abraham to leave Haran and continue to the land of Canaan. So Abraham went. At the same time, God made a promise to him. Although both Abraham and his wife Sarah were old and childless God said to him, 'I will make you into a great nation and I will bless you; I will make your name great, and you will be a blessing' (Genesis 12:2).

God's promise began to be fulfilled when Abraham was settled in Canaan at Mamre, near Hebron, and unexpectedly became the father of two sons – Ishmael, and then later, Isaac. Ishmael was 'the child of the flesh', as he was the son of Sarah's maid Hagar, and became the father of the Arabs. Isaac,

on the other hand, was 'the child of promise', born to Sarah, Abraham's wife, according to God's promise (Genesis 17:19–21). It was through Isaac that the Hebrew line of descent was continued.

Isaac, who married Rebekah, also had two sons – Esau and Jacob. But it was Jacob who, by depriving Esau of his birthright and deceitfully obtaining his father's blessing, became the third Hebrew Patriarch whilst Esau became the father of the Edomites.

After deceiving his father, Jacob left Canaan and went to Haran in Mesopotamia. There he worked for his uncle, Laban, for some years, and also married Laban's two daughters – Leah and Rachel. By the time he returned to Canaan, Jacob had twelve sons whose descendants became the twelve tribes of Israel.

The lowest level of the vast Ziggurat at Ur, Iraq. It covers an area of 62.5 by 43 metres

Abraham's well, Beersheba

Rachel's Tomb, Bethlehem

Jacob's favourite son, Joseph, was sold as a slave by his jealous brothers, and taken to Egypt where he was eventually imprisoned. In prison, Joseph interpreted the dreams of two other prisoners who were servants of the Pharaoh of Egypt. Later, Pharaoh himself had two dreams which no one could interpret. So he sent for Joseph who explained that his dreams meant there would be seven years of great plenty in Egypt followed by seven years of severe famine. Joseph also advised Pharaoh to appoint a wise man to store grain during the seven plentiful years in preparation for the famine. The result was that Pharaoh appointed Joseph to organise the storage of grain, and made him governor of Egypt.

During the famine, which affected Canaan as well as Egypt, Jacob sent his eleven other sons to Egypt to buy grain. Eventually, when Joseph had made himself known to his brothers, Jacob and his family migrated from Canaan to Egypt where they prospered and multiplied. They became so numerous and strong that a later Pharaoh – possibly Rameses II (1290–1224 BC) – made them slaves (Exodus 1:8–11).

Mosque at Hebron where the Patriarchs are buried

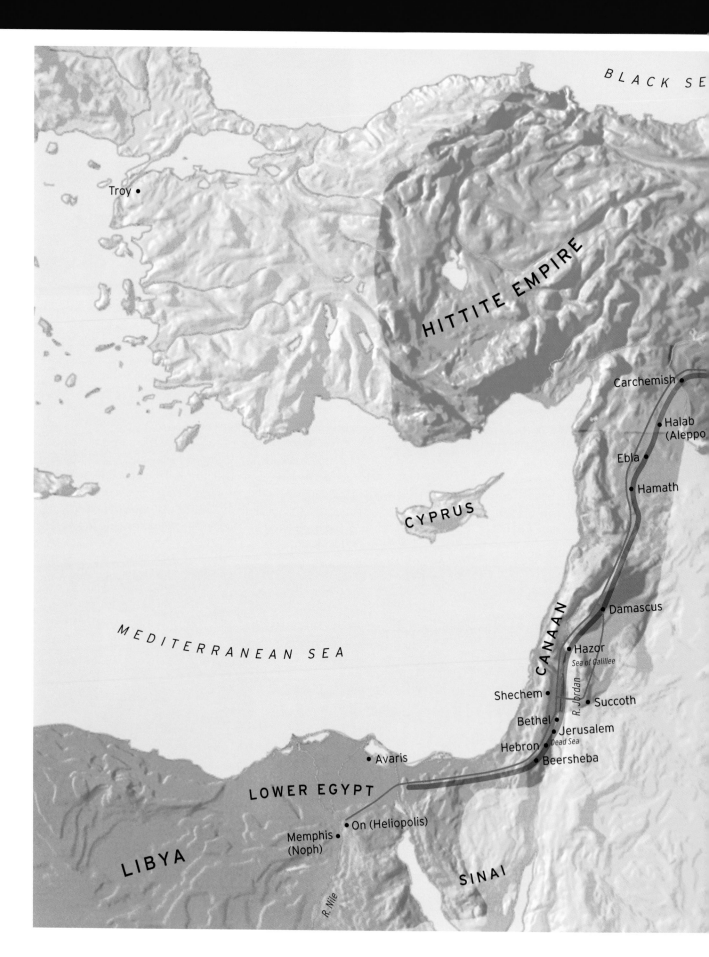

BLACK SEA

Troy •

HITTITE EMPIRE

Carchemish •

Halab
(Aleppo)

Ebla •

Hamath •

CYPRUS

MEDITERRANEAN SEA

Damascus •

CANAAN

Hazor •
Sea of Galilee

Shechem •

R. Jordan

Succoth •

Bethel •

Jerusalem •

Hebron •
Dead Sea

Beersheba •

Avaris •

LOWER EGYPT

On (Heliopolis) •

Memphis
(Noph) •

LIBYA

SINAI

R. Nile

14

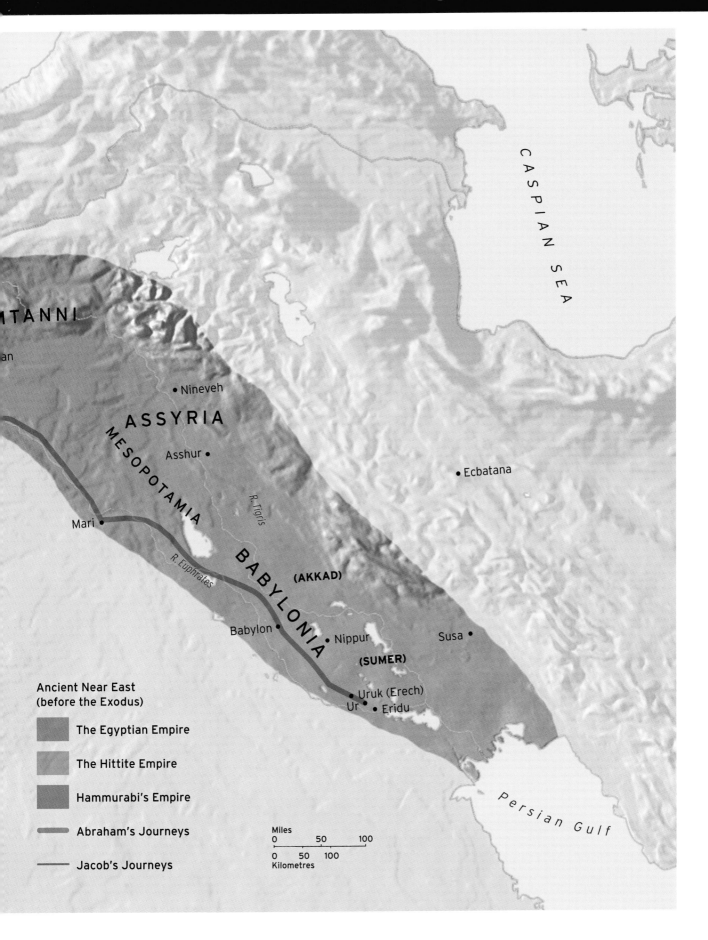

CASPIAN SEA

MITANNI

• Nineveh

ASSYRIA

Asshur •

• Ecbatana

MESOPOTAMIA

R. Tigris

Mari •

R. Euphrates

BABYLONIA

(AKKAD)

Babylon • • Nippur Susa •

(SUMER)

Uruk (Erech)
Ur • • Eridu

Ancient Near East
(before the Exodus)

The Egyptian Empire

The Hittite Empire

Hammurabi's Empire

Abraham's Journeys

Jacob's Journeys

Miles
0   50   100

0   50   100
Kilometres

Persian Gulf

WHEN the Hebrews had been in Egypt for about four hundred years God called Moses to free them from their slavery and lead them back to the promised land of Canaan (Exodus 3). Eventually, after Egypt had been afflicted by a series of plagues, they miraculously escaped from the Egyptians by crossing the Sea of Reeds (or Red Sea) on dry land into the Sinai desert (Exodus 14). This great event in the history of the Hebrews is known as the Exodus, and possibly took place during the reign of the Pharaoh Merneptah (1224–1216 BC). But it was not until forty years later, according to the biblical accounts, that the Hebrews entered the promised land. During the intervening years they were 'wandering in the wilderness'.

Sphinx and Cheop's pyramid at Giza, Egypt

The exact route taken by Moses and the Hebrews from Egypt to Canaan is uncertain because the biblical accounts are confusing, and many of the places mentioned have not yet been identified. But the traditional route is shown on the map (overleaf). This places the crossing of the sea at the southern end of Lake Menzaleh. After entering the wilderness of the Sinai desert, God led Moses to take an indirect, southerly, route to Canaan in order to avoid a number of Egyptian fortresses which guarded the direct easterly route known as 'The Way to the Land of the Philistines'.

A southerly route is also based on the ancient tradition that Mount Sinai, where Moses received the Law from God (Exodus 19–25), is the present-day Jebel Musa (the mountain of Moses) in the south of the Sinai peninsula. Certainly, Christian hermits were living on this mountain as early as the fourth century AD, and in the sixth century AD the emperor Justinian built the famous monastery of St Catherine here, which is still occupied by Christian monks.

From Mount Sinai the Hebrews travelled in a north-easterly direction through the wilderness of the Sinai desert to the oasis of Kadesh Barnea, a site which has been identified south of the Negev desert. Moses evidently planned to

Statue of Rameses II at Karnak, Egypt

16

invade Canaan from Kadesh Barnea because it was from here that he sent twelve men to spy out the land.

The spies discovered that the land was indeed 'flowing with milk and honey', but occupied by people living in strong, fortified cities (Numbers 13–14). When the Hebrews heard their discouraging report they were too frightened to enter Canaan, and remained at Kadesh Barnea for some time. Moses then decided to invade Canaan from the east. But the king of Edom refused to give Moses permission to travel north along the King's Highway, the main trade route from Ezion Geber to Damascus (Numbers 20:14–21).

Once again the Hebrews were forced to resume their wanderings. They went from Kadesh Barnea to Mount Hor, where Aaron died, and then turned south to Ezion Geber before taking a route north to avoid passing through Edom and Moab. But when Sihon, king of the Amorites, refused to allow them

to travel through his kingdom a battle was fought at Jahaz. Sihon was killed and his territory captured. The Hebrews then moved further north along the King's Highway to Bashan where they fought and defeated the giant king Og at the battle of Edrei (Deuteronomy 2:26–3:11).

The result of these victories was that the Hebrews occupied the east bank of the River Jordan – from Mount Hermon in the north to the River Arnon in the south. They were now in a position to invade Canaan itself, and Moses gathered his people together on the plains of Moab in preparation for the advance. But Moses was denied the joy of leading them into Canaan himself. After viewing the promised land from the summit of Mount Nebo and appointing Joshua his successor, he died (Deuteronomy 34:1–7).

Wadi Musa (The Fountain of Moses) Jordan

Mount Hor – traditional burial place of Aaron (Jordan)

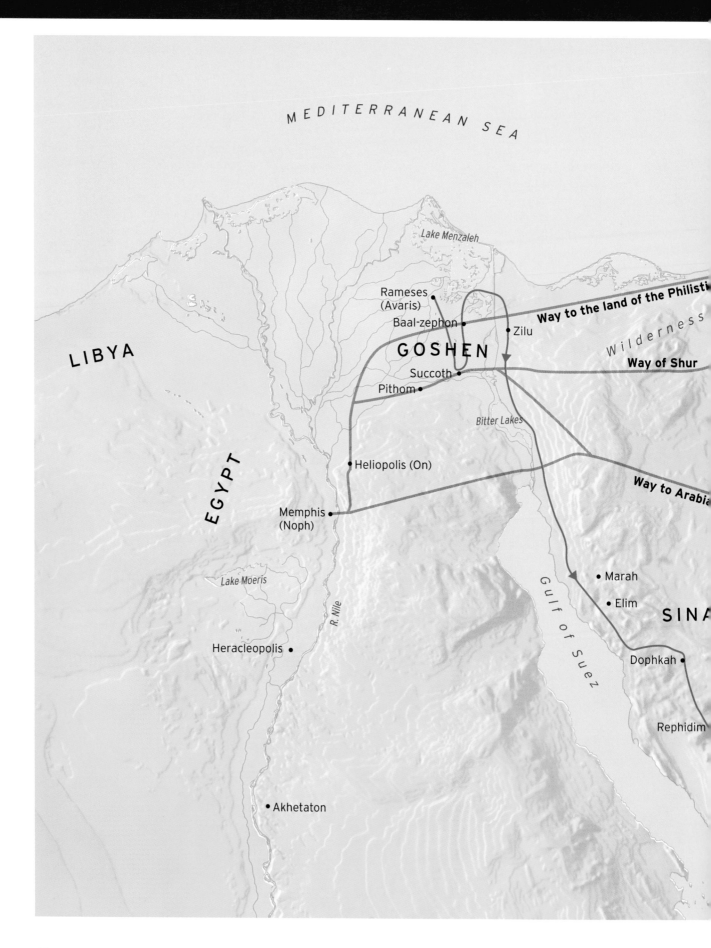

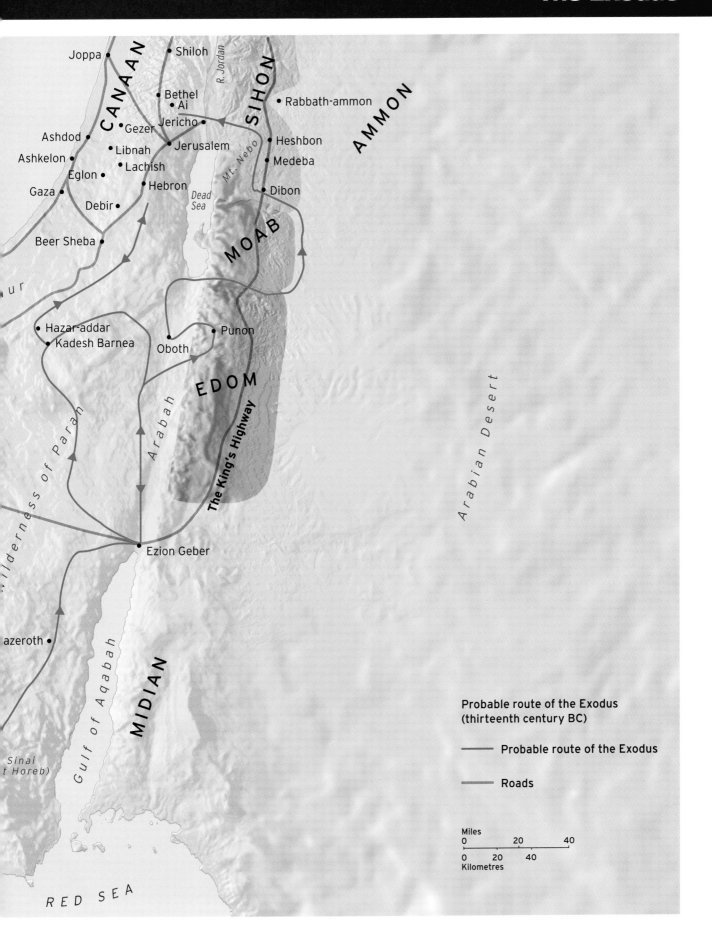

Joppa •   • Shiloh

CANAAN

SIHON

R. Jordan

Bethel •
• Ai

• Rabbath-ammon

AMMON

Gezer •
Ashdod •
Jericho •

• Jerusalem

Heshbon •
Medeba •

Ashkelon •
• Libnah

Eglon •
• Lachish

Mt. Nebo

Gaza •
• Hebron

Dead
Sea

• Dibon

Debir •

MOAB

Beer Sheba •

...ur

• Hazar-addar
• Kadesh Barnea

• Punon

Oboth

Arabah

EDOM

Wilderness of Paran

The King's Highway

Ezion Geber

Arabian Desert

...azeroth •

MIDIAN

Gulf of Aqabah

Sinai
(t Horeb)

**Probable route of the Exodus
(thirteenth century BC)**

——— Probable route of the Exodus

——— Roads

Miles
0   20   40

0   20   40
Kilometres

RED SEA

AFTER the death of Moses, God called Joshua to lead the Hebrews, or Israelites, into Canaan (Joshua 1:1–2). He sent two men to spy out Jericho, and then led the people of Israel from Moab across the river Jordan – when its waters were cut off between Adam and the Dead Sea – to Gilgal. After destroying Jericho and Ai, and defeating an alliance of five kings at Gibeon, Joshua conquered the south of the country. After defeating another alliance of kings in a battle at the Waters of Merom, he also destroyed the strategic city of Hazor and conquered the north of the country.

Joshua, however, did not succeed in conquering the entire land of Canaan, which was occupied not only by Canaanites but also by people of other races, including the Philistines. The Canaanites, for example, continued to occupy many important cities, and the Philistines remained in control of their five key cities: Gaza, Ashdod, Ashkelon, Gath and Ekron (Joshua 13:1–7). Nevertheless, Joshua divided up the land amongst the tribes. Reuben, Gad and half the tribe of Manasseh had already been allotted

the occupied land on the east bank of the Jordan (Joshua 14:3–4). Now, in Canaan, lots were cast at Gilgal and Shiloh for the division of the land amongst the other nine tribes and half the tribe of Manasseh, as shown on the map opposite (Joshua 14:6–19:48). Six cities of refuge were appointed (Joshua 20) and forty-eight cities were given to the Levites (Joshua 21:1–42). Finally, before he died, Joshua gathered all the tribes at Shechem and, like Moses at Mount Sinai, he made a covenant (or agreement) with his people who promised to be faithful in serving God (Joshua 24).

After the death of Joshua the Israelites not only continued to fight their enemies in Canaan, but also fought the people who attacked them from the east bank of the Jordan. Their leaders at this time were popular hero-deliverers called 'Judges' whose dramatic exploits are recorded in the book of Judges.

Ehud, for example, defeated the Moabites (Judges 3:12–30), and Deborah, with her army commander, Barak, won a decisive victory over the Canaanites (Judges 4–5). Gideon,

similarly, attacked and defeated the Midianites (Judges 6:1–8:28) and Jephthah slaughtered the Ammonites (Judges 10:17–11:33). But it was the Philistines who became the Israelites' most formidable foe. Their strength became apparent during the time of Samson, the last of the judges, whose many daring attacks against them ended in his death (Judges 13–16).

Petra, High place of Sacrifice (Jordan)

Remains of Old Testament Jericho

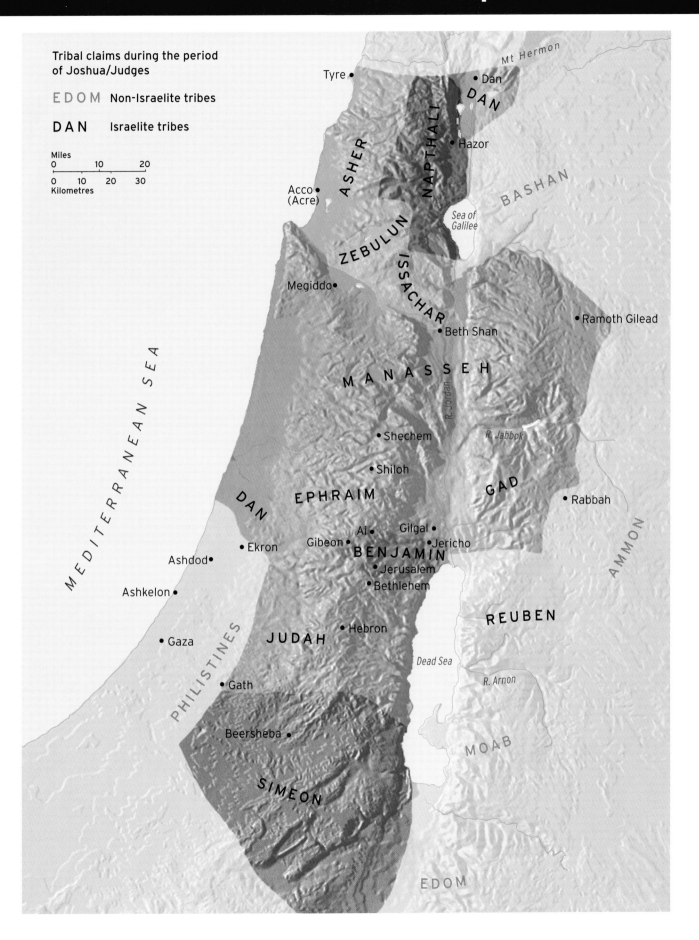

Tribal claims during the period
of Joshua/Judges

EDOM   Non-Israelite tribes

DAN   Israelite tribes

Miles
0   10   20

0   10   20   30
Kilometres

Tyre

Dan

DAN

Hazor

ASHER

NAPTHALI

BASHAN

Acco
(Acre)

Sea of
Galilee

ZEBULUN

ISSACHAR

Megiddo

Ramoth Gilead

Beth Shan

MANASSEH

R. Jordan

Shechem

R. Jabbok

Shiloh

MEDITERRANEAN SEA

DAN

EPHRAIM

GAD

Rabbah

Ekron

Ai   Gilgal

Gibeon   Jericho

BENJAMIN

AMMON

Ashdod

Jerusalem

Ashkelon

Bethlehem

REUBEN

Gaza

Hebron

JUDAH

Dead Sea

R. Arnon

PHILISTINES

Gath

MOAB

Beersheba

SIMEON

EDOM

Stone carving believd to be of the ark of the covenant, Capernaum

TOWARDS the end of the period of the Judges (around 1200–1020 BC) the Israelites were faced with a crisis. Their occupation of Canaan was threatened by the growing power of the Philistines who had already extended their territory eastwards.

During the time of Samuel, the Philistines defeated the Israelites in a battle at Ebenezer. The Israelites, in despair, then sent to the sanctuary at Shiloh for the sacred ark of the covenant in the hope that it would enable them to defeat the Philistines. But the Israelites were again defeated in a second major battle at Ebenezer, the Philistines slaughtering them in their thousands and also capturing the sacred ark (1 Samuel 4:1–11). However, when they were suddenly afflicted with a plague, the Philistines thought the ark was responsible and returned it to the Israelites at Beth Shemesh. From here, the Israelites took the ark to Kiriath Jearim where it remained for twenty years (1 Samuel 5:1–7:3).

After their great victory, the Philistines occupied much of Canaan. The Israelites then asked Samuel to appoint a king to rule over them, and lead them in their fight against their enemies (1 Samuel 8:4–22). The result was that Saul – a man from the tribe of Benjamin renowned for his bravery and great height – became the first Israelite king in about 1020 BC (1 Samuel 10:1–11:15).

The first battle which Saul fought and won was against the Ammonites at Jabesh Gilead, east of the Jordan (1 Samuel 11:1–13). Then, helped by Jonathan his son, he successfully attacked the Philistines at Michmash, north of Jerusalem, enabling him to drive them out of the central hill country (1 Samuel 14:1–46).

Although the Philistines continued to attack the Israelites throughout Saul's reign he managed to hold them in check and maintained his control over much of Canaan, as the map opposite shows, until the death of Samuel. Then, the Philistines gathered their forces at Aphek and advanced northwards to the Plain of Esdraelon where a major battle was fought. The Philistines inflicted a crushing defeat on the Israelites, and Saul committed suicide on nearby Mount Gilboa after three of his sons, including Jonathan, had been killed. Once again the triumphant Philistines controlled much of Canaan and also occupied land east of the Jordan.

Tell at Beth Shan

Plain of Esdraelon

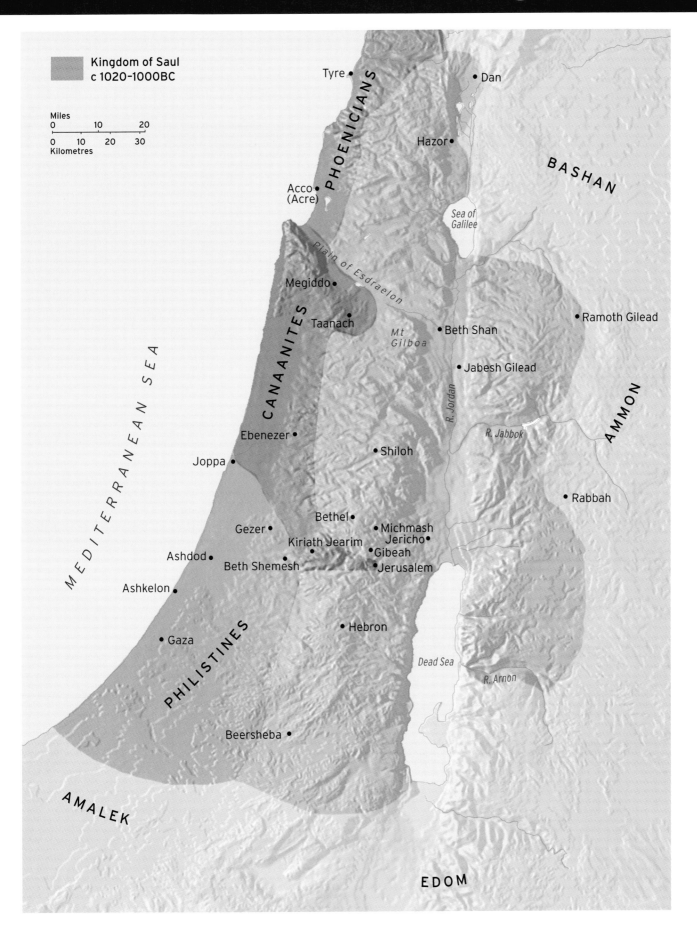

Kingdom of Saul
c 1020–1000BC

Miles
0   10   20

0   10   20   30
Kilometres

Tyre

Dan

PHOENICIANS

BASHAN

Hazor

Acco
(Acre)

Sea of
Galilee

Plain of Esdraelon

Megiddo

CANAANITES

Taanach

Mt
Gilboa

Beth Shan

Ramoth Gilead

Jabesh Gilead

R. Jordan

R. Jabbok

AMMON

Ebenezer

MEDITERRANEAN SEA

Shiloh

Joppa

Rabbah

Bethel

Gezer

Michmash
Jericho

Kiriath Jearim

Gibeah

Ashdod

Beth Shemesh

Jerusalem

Ashkelon

Hebron

PHILISTINES

Gaza

Dead Sea

R. Arnon

Beersheba

AMALEK

EDOM

AFTER the death of Saul, Ish-Bosheth, one of his sons, became king of the northern tribes of Israel at Mahanaim, east of the Jordan (2 Samuel 2:8–10). But David, who rose to prominence during Saul's reign, was proclaimed king of the southern tribe of Judah at Hebron (2 Samuel 2:1–4). However, about 1000 BC, after the murder of Ish-Bosheth, David became king of all Israel (2 Samuel 4:5–5:5) and a new era in the history of the Israelites began. For under David, the northern tribes of Israel and the southern tribe of Judah first became a nation, forming a strong, united kingdom.

Stone terraces dating from David's time, Jerusalem

Excavations of Megiddo

Meanwhile, after reigning in Hebron for seven years, David captured the strategic Jebusite city of Jerusalem, and made it his new capital (2 Samuel 5:6–8). He also made Jerusalem the religious, as well as the political, capital of his kingdom by bringing the sacred ark from Kiriath Jearim to the city (2 Samuel 6; 1 Chronicles 13:1–14). So Jerusalem, the city of David, also became the Holy City of God.

David's swift rise to power, however, soon alarmed the Philistines who gathered a great army near Jerusalem to overthrow him. But David defeated them so decisively in two major battles that their power was broken, and they never again became a serious threat to Israel (2 Samuel 5:17–25). He then attacked and conquered the nations east of the Jordan, and extended his kingdom from the river Euphrates to the borders of Egypt (2 Samuel 8:3). But towards the end of his reign two unsuccessful attempts were made to topple David from his throne, firstly by Absalom, a favourite son of David's (2 Samuel 15:1–22). Then, shortly before David died, Adonijah, his oldest surviving son, tried to obtain the throne. But David appointed Solomon, his son by Bathsheba, to succeed him as king (1 Kings 1).

Solomon's reign (around 961–922 BC) was a time of peace and prosperity for Israel, and renowned for the splendour and glory of his achievements. He did not attempt to extend the empire which he had inherited, but strengthened it by making alliances with neighbouring countries, and engaging in world-wide trade, which greatly increased his wealth. Solomon also carried out a vast building programme, which included the magnificent first Temple in Jerusalem, royal palaces, and the fortified cities of Hazor, Megiddo and Gezer. But towards the end of his reign Solomon forsook the faith of his forefathers, and his oppressive rule resulted in discontent and revolt amongst his subjects (1 Kings 11).

A view of Hebron

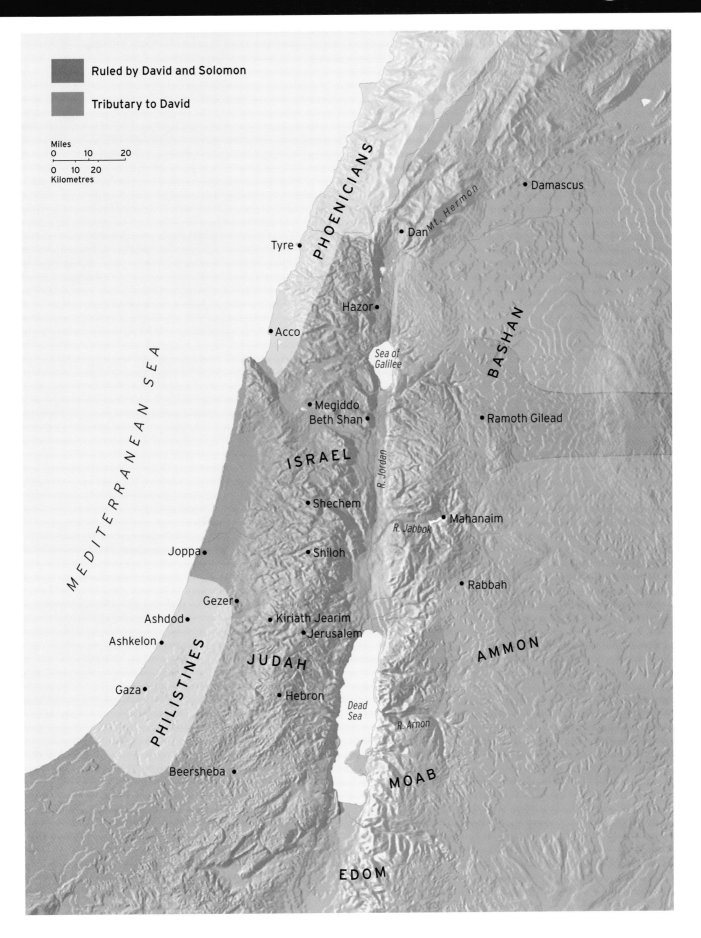

Ruled by David and Solomon

Tributary to David

Miles
0   10   20
0   10   20
Kilometres

PHOENICIANS

• Damascus

• Dan Mt. Hermon

Tyre •

Hazor •

• Acco

Sea of
Galilee

BASHAN

• Megiddo
Beth Shan •

• Ramoth Gilead

ISRAEL

• Shechem

R. Jordan

• Mahanaim

R. Jabbok

Joppa •

• Shiloh

MEDITERRANEAN SEA

Gezer •

Ashdod •

• Kiriath Jearim

• Jerusalem

• Rabbah

Ashkelon •

PHILISTINES

JUDAH

AMMON

Gaza •

• Hebron

Dead
Sea

R. Arnon

Beersheba •

MOAB

EDOM

WHEN Solomon died, about 922 BC, the tension and discontent amongst the people led to the permanent division of his kingdom. The ten northern tribes broke away from the Dynasty of David to form the kingdom of Israel. Their first king was Jeroboam, a man from the tribe of Ephraim who had previously led an unsuccessful revolt against Solomon (1 Kings 11:26–40). He made his capital at Shechem, which was later moved to Tirzah and then to Samaria (1 Kings 16:24). The two southern tribes of Judah and Benjamin, however, remained faithful to the Dynasty of David. They formed the kingdom of Judah under King Rehoboam, Solomon's son, whose capital was at Jerusalem (1 Kings 14:21).

The political separation of the two kingdoms was also accompanied by a religious division. For, as Solomon's Temple at Jerusalem was now situated in Judah, Jeroboam built two rival temples in Israel – at Dan in the north and Bethel in the south. In each temple he set up a golden statue of a bull-calf (1 Kings 12:25–33).

Jeroboam is strongly condemned in the Bible because 'he caused Israel to sin' by promoting and encouraging idolatry amongst the people. But he was not the only king during the period of the Divided Kingdom to lead his people astray from the true worship of Yahweh. The prophet Elijah, for example, opposed Ahab of Israel and his wife Jezebel because they promoted the worship of the pagan god Baal (1 Kings 18). Later prophets – such as Amos and Hosea in Israel, and Isaiah and Jeremiah in Judah – condemned pagan worship too, and tried to lead the people back to the true worship of Yahweh. They also condemned the social evils in their countries, and often opposed the political policies of their kings.

During the period of their separation the two kingdoms were frequently at war with each other, which made them an easy prey to attacks from neighbouring countries. Both kingdoms, for example, fought the Egyptians, Moabites and Syrians, and Judah also fought the Philistines, Ammonites and Edomites. But in the middle of the eighth century BC they faced their most powerful enemy: the mighty empire of Assyria. In 722 BC the Assyrians finally conquered and occupied the northern kingdom, Israel, which ended the period of the Divided Kingdom.

Excavations at Dan

Statue of Elijah at Muhraqa on Mount Carmel

Tower of the West Gate, Samaria

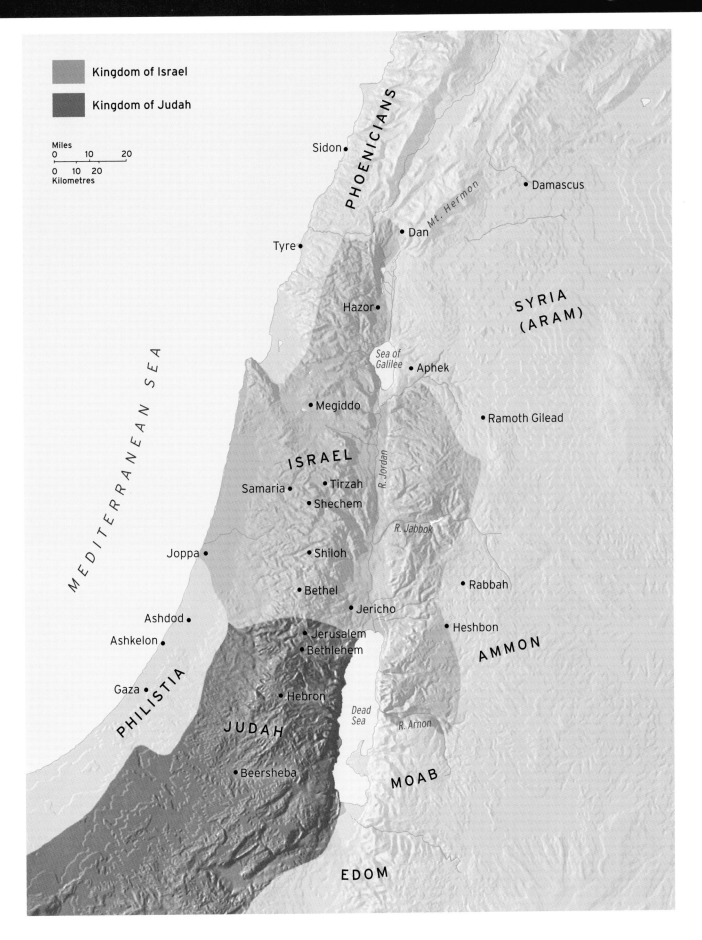

Kingdom of Israel

Kingdom of Judah

Miles
0   10   20

0   10   20
Kilometres

PHOENICIANS

Sidon•

•Damascus

Tyre•

•Dan   *Mt. Hermon*

Hazor•

SYRIA
(ARAM)

*Sea of
Galilee* •Aphek

•Megiddo

•Ramoth Gilead

ISRAEL

R. Jordan

Samaria•   •Tirzah
    •Shechem

R. Jabbok

Joppa•   •Shiloh

•Rabbah

•Bethel

    •Jericho

Ashdod•   •Heshbon

Ashkelon•   •Jerusalem
      •Bethlehem   AMMON

M E D I T E R R A N E A N   S E A

Gaza•   PHILISTIA

    •Hebron

*Dead
Sea*   *R. Arnon*

JUDAH

•Beersheba   MOAB

EDOM

Remains of Ziggurat, Nimrud (Iraq)

IT WAS during the period of the Divided Kingdom that the Assyrians established their great empire, which eventually stretched from Mesopotamia to Egypt.

After extending their frontiers in the east, the Assyrian kings turned their armies against the west, bringing Israel and Judah onto the stage of world history. They first conquered Syria and received tribute from Israel. Tiglath-Pileser III (745–727 BC) then occupied a large part of Israel, but Hoshea was allowed to rule the remaining territory from Samaria, the capital, as a vassal king. Hoshea, however, rebelled against Assyria during the reign of Shalmaneser V (727–722 BC), who invaded his territory and besieged Samaria. The siege lasted three years, and Samaria finally fell in 722 BC, during the reign of Sargon II (722–705 BC), bringing the kingdom of Israel to an end. Sargon deported the people to Assyria, which is the last we hear of the 'lost ten tribes of Israel'. He then replaced them with foreign settlers who were later known as Samaritans (2 Kings 17:5–6,24).

Boat on the River Euphrates

Meanwhile, although Judah had been an Assyrian vassal-state since the time of Tiglath-Pileser, they had escaped invasion. But when Hezekiah (715–687 BC) rebelled against Assyria, Sennacherib (705–681 BC) attacked Judah. While he was blockading Jerusalem, however, his army was stricken with a plague and Sennacherib suddenly withdrew to Nineveh, his capital (see 2 Kings 19:35). Jerusalem escaped destruction and Judah survived. But her days were numbered: less than a century later the Assyrian Empire fell to the Babylonians, which sealed the fate of Judah.

Site of Asshur on the River Tigris

Relief of Assurnasirpal, Nimrud

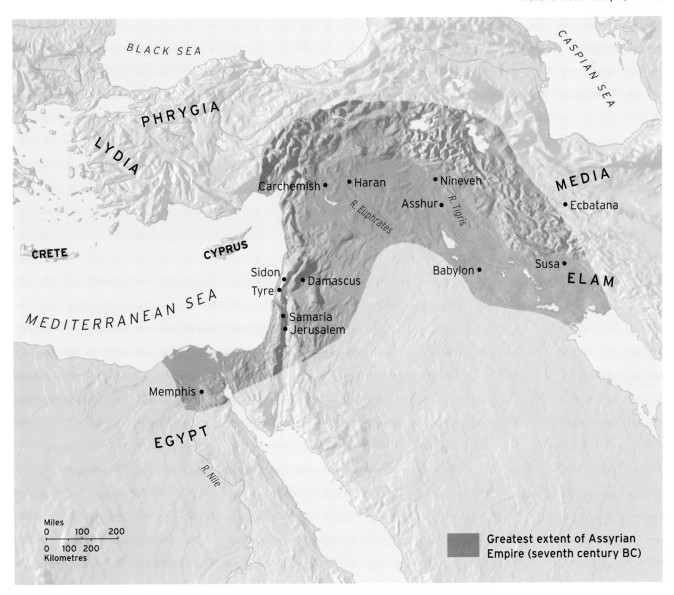

BLACK SEA

CASPIAN SEA

PHRYGIA

LYDIA

MEDIA

Carchemish • • Haran • Nineveh

Asshur • Ecbatana

R. Euphrates *R. Tigris*

CRETE

CYPRUS

Sidon • Babylon • Susa •

Tyre • • Damascus ELAM

MEDITERRANEAN SEA

• Samaria
• Jerusalem

Memphis •

EGYPT

R. Nile

Miles
0   100   200

0   100 200
Kilometres

Greatest extent of Assyrian
Empire (seventh century BC)

ASSYRIA reached the peak of its power during the reign of Ashurbanipal (668–630 BC). After his death, however, the great empire soon fell to the Medes and Babylonians, who destroyed Nineveh, the capital, in 612 BC and finally defeated the Assyrians at Haran in 609 BC.

Meanwhile, Josiah of Judah (640–609 BC) had tried to prevent Pharaoh Neco of Egypt from going to the aid of the Assyrians. But Neco defeated and killed Josiah at Megiddo (2 Kings 23:29–30). He occupied Syria and Palestine for a short while before his army was annihilated by the Babylonians under Nebuchadnezzar (605–562 BC) at Carchemish in 605 BC. Judah then became a Babylonian vassal state. But it was not long before Nebuchadnezzar had to put down a revolt. In 597 BC he attacked Jerusalem, deported a large number of people to Babylon, and appointed Zedekiah as a vassal king (2 Kings 24). But he, too, rebelled – in spite of warnings from the prophet Jeremiah. Once again, Nebuchadnezzar attacked Judah. In 587 BC he destroyed the entire city of Jerusalem, including Solomon's Temple, and once more deported many people to Babylon. Among them was Zedekiah, who was replaced by a governor, Gedaliah, who was soon murdered. Most of the remaining people, accompanied by Jeremiah, then fled to Egypt. This was the end of the kingdom of Judah (2 Kings 25).

The Lion of Babylon dates from Nebuchadnezzar's reign

Excavations and reconstructed E-Makh Temple at Babylon, Iraq

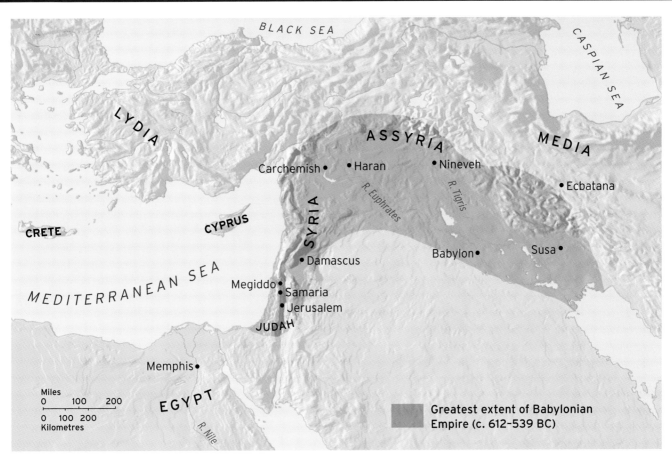

BLACK SEA

CASPIAN SEA

LYDIA

ASSYRIA

MEDIA

Carchemish •   • Haran   • Nineveh

• Ecbatana

R. Euphrates

R. Tigris

SYRIA

CRETE   CYPRUS

• Damascus

Babylon •   • Susa

MEDITERRANEAN SEA

Megiddo •
         • Samaria
         • Jerusalem

JUDAH

Memphis •

EGYPT

R. Nile

Miles
0   100   200

0   100 200
Kilometres

Greatest extent of Babylonian
Empire (c. 612–539 BC)

Nebuchadnezzar II's
Palace, Babylon, Iraq

Remains of the Ishtar Gate, Babylon

Reconstruction of the Ishtar Gate, Babylon

Tomb of Cyrus at Pasargadae, Iran

Gate of Xerxes in Persepolis, Iran

THE story of the Jews begins when the people of Judah were deported to Babylon for, unlike the people of Israel, the people of Judah retained their national identity and religion during their exile. Much of the Old Testament was also written down at this time.

The Jews remained in exile until the Babylonian Empire was conquered by Cyrus, the founder of the vast Persian Empire which, as the map opposite shows, eventually stretched from India to Macedonia. Cyrus was hailed as 'The Lord's Anointed' (Isaiah 45:1), and after capturing Babylon in 539 BC, he gave the Jews permission to return to Judah and rebuild the Temple in Jerusalem. Many, but not all, the Jews returned to Judah. But the rebuilding of the Temple was not completed until 515 BC, during the time of the prophets Haggai and Zechariah.

Later, during the fifth century BC, Ezra, a priest, returned from Babylon with another group of exiles and reorganised the religious life of the Jews (Ezra 7:1–10:17). At about the same time the walls of Jerusalem were rebuilt by Nehemiah, the Jewish governor (Nehemiah 2–7). He also carried out a number of social reforms (Nehemiah 13). Little is known of the history of the Jews during the rest of the Persian period, which ended when Alexander the Great of Macedon conquered the Persian Empire in 333 BC.

Rock Tomb of Xerxes at Naqsh-i-Rostem, Iran

Tomb of Daniel at Susa, Iran

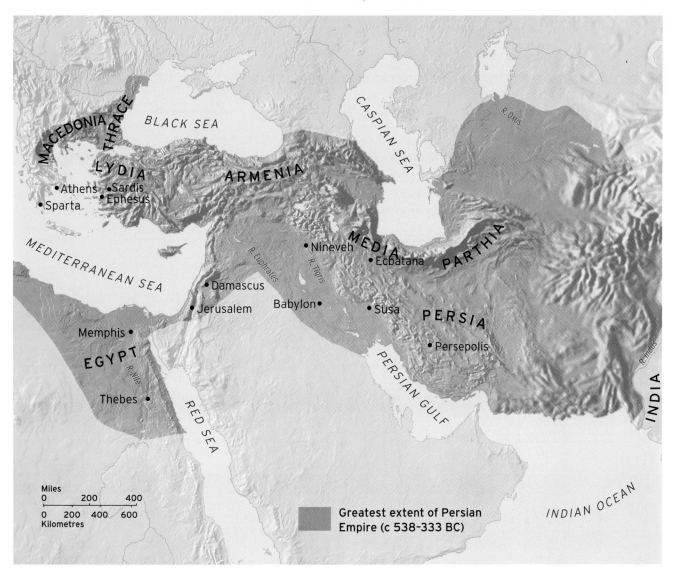

MACEDONIA

THRACE

BLACK SEA

CASPIAN SEA

R. Oxus

LYDIA

ARMENIA

•Athens •Sardis
•Ephesus

•Sparta

MEDITERRANEAN SEA

MEDIA

PARTHIA

•Nineveh

•Ecbatana

R. Euphrates

R. Tigris

•Damascus

•Jerusalem

Babylon•

•Susa

PERSIA

Memphis •

EGYPT

•Persepolis

R. Nile

PERSIAN GULF

INDIA

R. Indus

Thebes •

RED SEA

INDIAN OCEAN

Miles
0   200   400

0   200   400   600
Kilometres

Greatest extent of Persian
Empire (c 538-333 BC)

DURING his campaigns against the Persians, Alexander the Great took control of Palestine. But when he died at Babylon in 323 BC his great empire was divided into three kingdoms under three rival dynasties. Macedonia was ruled by Antigonus, Egypt by the Ptolemies, and Syria by the Seleucids.

The Ptolemies of Egypt first controlled Palestine for over a century, until 198 BC. Then the Seleucid king of Syria, Antiochus III (223–187 BC) defeated Ptolemy V at Paneas, near the sources of the river Jordan, and added Palestine to his empire.

During their occupation of Palestine the Seleucids tried to impose the Greek way of life and the Greek religion on the Jews – with some success. But in 167 BC Antiochus IV, known as Antiochus Epiphanes (175–163 BC), desecrated the Temple in Jerusalem and prohibited the Jews from practising their religion. This attack on the Jewish religion led to the Maccabean rebellion.

Under the Maccabees the Jews not only regained their religious freedom but also achieved a brief period of political independence. This lasted from 142 BC until the Romans conquered Palestine in 63 BC. The Maccabean period, however, was marred by disputes which arose at this time between two Jewish religious sects, the Pharisees and Sadducees. A third sect, the Essenes, was also established during this period, and some of them almost certainly lived at Qumran on the shores of the Dead Sea. But little was known about the Essenes until 1947 when the famous Dead Sea Scrolls were first discovered hidden in caves near their monastery, which has now been excavated.

Maccabean Tomb, known as 'Absalom's Tomb', Jerusalem

Temple of Horus at Edfu, Egypt

Maccabean Tower, Jerusalem

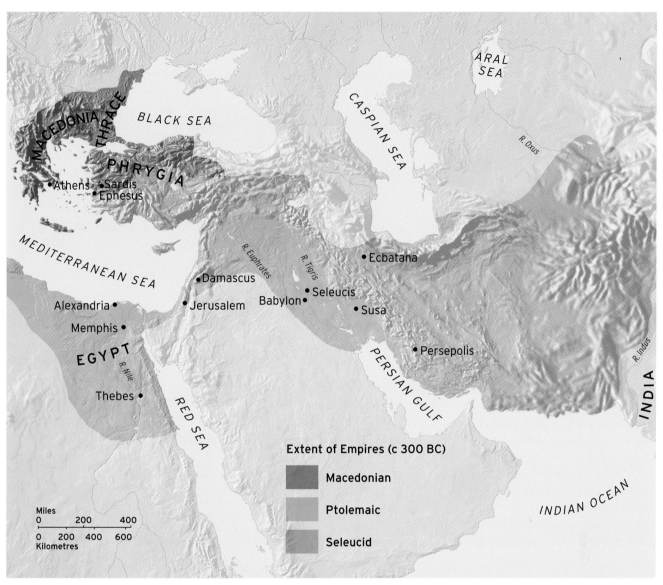

ARAL SEA

BLACK SEA

CASPIAN SEA

R. Oxus

MACEDONIA

THRACE

PHRYGIA

• Athens • Sardis
  • Ephesus

MEDITERRANEAN SEA

R. Euphrates

R. Tigris

• Ecbatana

• Damascus

Alexandria •

• Jerusalem

Babylon • • Seleucis

• Susa

Memphis •

EGYPT

R. Nile

• Persepolis

PERSIAN GULF

R. Indus

INDIA

Thebes •

RED SEA

INDIAN OCEAN

Extent of Empires (c 300 BC)

Macedonian

Ptolemaic

Seleucid

Miles
0   200   400

0   200 400 600
Kilometres

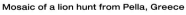

Mosaic of a lion hunt from Pella, Greece

Temple of Apollo at Corinth, Greece

Towards the end of the Maccabean period, the Romans began to extend their rule in the East. The Roman general Pompey took control of Syria, marched into Palestine, and captured Jerusalem in 63 BC, after a three-month siege. The Jews in Palestine then lost their short-lived independence for over 2,000 years – until 1948 when the present State of Israel was founded.

At first, the Roman governor of Syria controlled Palestine. Then in 55 BC Julius Caesar made Antipater, an Idumean, procurator of Judea. When Antipater was murdered in 43 BC, the Roman Senate appointed Herod, one of Antipater's sons, king of the Jews. Known as Herod the Great, he ruled the Jews under the Romans for thirty-three years, from 37 to 4 BC.

During his long reign Herod undertook numerous building projects in Palestine and elsewhere. Remains of his magnificent cities, palaces and fortresses can still be seen in the Holy Land today, for example at Caesarea, Masada and Samaria, as well as in Jerusalem. Here, in an attempt to please the Jews, Herod began his most ambitious project: the rebuilding of the Temple. But Herod was a cruel and ruthless king and the Jews hated him.

Nevertheless, it was during Herod's reign that God's preparation of the world for the birth of Jesus was completed. For, by this time, God had not only prepared the Jews for this great event, He had also prepared other nations so that the message of Christianity – the religion founded by Jesus – could be spread throughout the world. This was made possible because the Greeks had provided the world with a common language, and the Romans had established universal peace throughout their great empire, together with a remarkable network of roads. So, as Paul wrote later, '... when the time had fully come, God sent his Son, born of woman ...' (Galatians 4:4).

The Jewish woman whom God chose to be the mother of Jesus was the Virgin Mary (Luke 1:26–38). Like Abraham, she was faithful to her divine calling, and Jesus was born at Bethlehem in Judea (Luke 2:1–7). The exact date of His birth is not known, but it was about 6 BC, before the death of Herod in 4 BC (Matthew 2:13–16). These dates are confusing because in the sixth century AD a monk who fixed the Christian calendar to begin in AD 1 made an error of about six years.

When Herod died his kingdom was divided between three of his surviving sons: Archelaus ruled over Judea, Samaria and Idumea; Herod Antipas ruled over Galilee and Perea; and Philip ruled over Iturea and Traconitis (Luke 3:1). But the Romans deposed Archelaus in AD 6 and placed his territory under the rule of procurators. One of them was Pontius Pilate (AD 26–36), who condemned Jesus to death.

Model of Herod's Temple, Jerusalem

The Forum of Rome, Italy

Later, Palestine was once more united for a short while under King Herod Agrippa I (AD 41–44), Herod the Great's grandson. But when he died, Roman procurators again ruled most of the country. Among them were Felix and Festus, under whom Paul was a prisoner (Acts 23–27).

When Florus (AD 64–66) was procurator, the First Jewish Revolt against the Romans broke out. This was crushed by Titus when he destroyed Jerusalem and burnt the Temple in AD 70 (cf. Luke 19:41–44). In AD 135 a Second Jewish Revolt was also crushed. The emperor Hadrian (AD 117–138) then built a Roman city called Aelia Capitolina on the ruins of Jerusalem, which the Jews were forbidden to enter for two hundred years.

Mosaic of a Roman chariot at Ostia, Italy

Roman aqueduct at Caesarea

Statue of Augustus Caesar, Rome

The fortress of Masada, used by Herod the Great

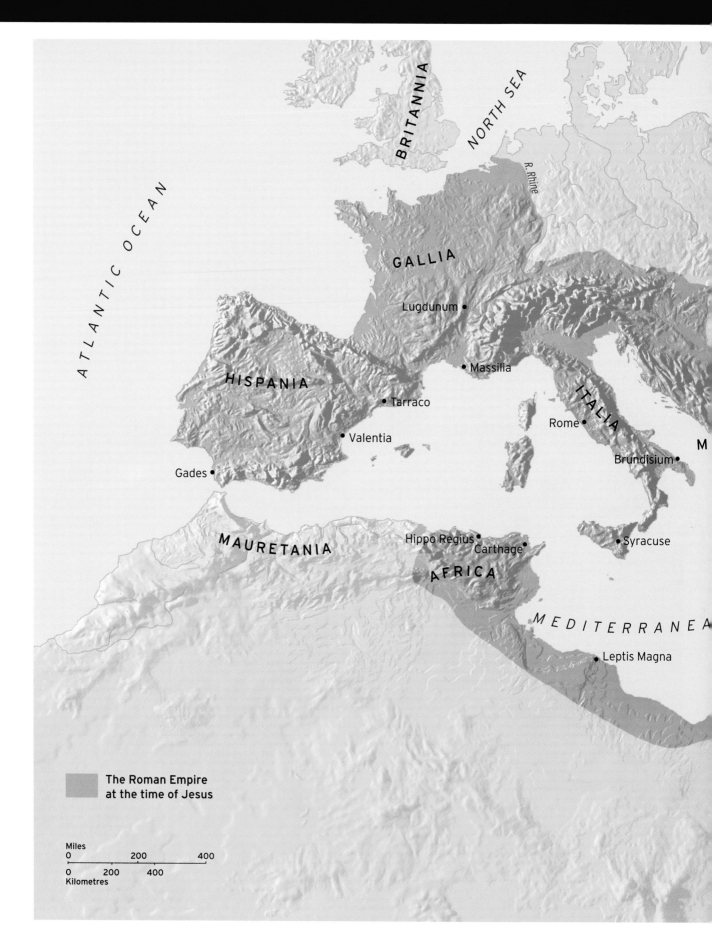

ATLANTIC OCEAN

BRITANNIA

NORTH SEA

R. Rhine

GALLIA

Lugdunum •

• Massilia

HISPANIA

• Tarraco

ITALIA

Rome •

• Valentia

Brundisium •

M

Gades •

MAURETANIA

Hippo Regius • • Syracuse

Carthage •

AFRICA

MEDITERRANEA

• Leptis Magna

The Roman Empire
at the time of Jesus

Miles
0   200   400

0   200   400
Kilometres

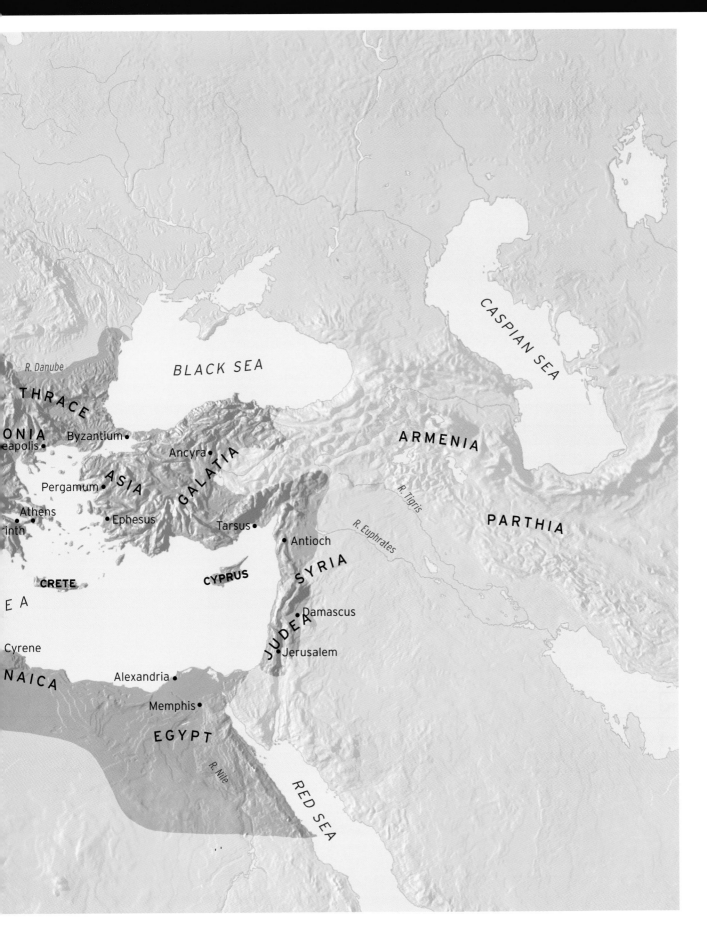

R. Danube

BLACK SEA

CASPIAN SEA

THRACE

ONIA

eapolis•

Byzantium•

Ancyra•

ARMENIA

ASIA

GALATIA

Pergamum•

R. Tigris

PARTHIA

Athens•

Ephesus

R. Euphrates

inth

Tarsus•

•Antioch

CYPRUS

SYRIA

CRETE

E A

•Damascus

JUDEA

Cyrene

•Jerusalem

NAICA

Alexandria•

Memphis•

EGYPT

R. Nile

RED SEA

BC	THE HEBREWS AND PALESTINE		THE EMPIRES
9000	Jericho occupied		
3500			Mesopotamia: Kingdom of Sumer
3100			Egypt: Upper and Lower Kingdoms united
3000			Mesopotamia invaded by Semitic tribes
2700–2200			Egypt: The Old Kingdom. Pyramids built
2400			Syria: Canaanite Empire of Ebla
2350–2200			Mesopotamia: Kingdom of Akkad
2250			Syria: Ebla destroyed by Narum-Sin of Akkad
2200			Mesopotamia invaded by Gutians
2100–1750			Egypt: The Middle Kingdom
2000			Mesopotamia invaded by Amorites
2000–1750	Hebrew Patriarchs in Palestine		
1890			Mesopotamia: old Babylonian Empire
1792			Hammurabi King of Babylon
			Mari destroyed by Hammurabi
1750			Egypt invaded by Hyksos
			Joseph rises to power in Egypt
	Jacob and his family migrate to Egypt		
1550			Egypt: Hyksos expelled
1550–1080			Egypt: The New Kingdom
1500			Mesopotamia invaded by the Horites
			Kingdom of Mitanni
1475–1200			Asia Minor: Hittite New Kingdom
1400–1200			Syria: Canaanite City-state of Ugarit
1290–1224	Hebrews in bondage in Egypt		Rameses II Pharaoh of Egypt
1224–1216	Exodus from Egypt		Merneptah Pharaoh of Egypt
	Palestine invaded by the Hebrews under Joshua		
1200–1020	Period of the Judges		
1190	Coastal plain of Palestine occupied by the Philistines		
1050	Battle of Ebenezer		
	Philistines defeated Israelites		
1020–1000	Saul is king		
1000–961	David is king. The United Kingdom		
961–922	Solomon is king		

	JUDAH	ISRAEL	ASSYRIAN EMPIRE
922	Rehoboam	Jeroboam I	
883			Ashurnasirpal II
876		Omri	
873	Jehoshaphat		
861		Ahab	
859			Shalmaneser III
853			Battle of Qarqar
842		Jehu	
786		Jeroboam II	
783	Uzziah		
745			Tiglath-Pileser III
732		Hoshea	
727			Shalmaneser V

Time Chart for the Old Testament Period

BC	THE HEBREWS AND PALESTINE		THE EMPIRES
	JUDAH	**ISRAEL**	**ASSYRIAN EMPIRE**
722		Fall of Samaria and the end of the Kingdom of Israel.	Sargon II
715	Hezekiah		
705			Sennacherib
687	Manasseh		
668			Ashurbanipal
640	Josiah		
612			Fall of Nineveh
609			Fall of Haran
			BABYLONIAN EMPIRE
605	Jerusalem taken by Nebuchadnezzar. Many Jews exiled including Ezekiel.		Battle of Carchemish at which the Egyptians were defeated.
597	Zedekiah		
587	Fall of Jerusalem Babylonian exile		
539			Fall of Babylon
			PERSIAN EMPIRE
538	First return of exiles		Cyrus
520–515	Rebuilding of the Temple		
522			Darius I
486			Xerxes I
465			Artaxerxes I
458	Return of Ezra		
445	Arrival of Nehemiah Rebuilding of Jerusalem's walls		
333			**EMPIRE OF ALEXANDER THE GREAT**
323			**PTOLEMAIC AND SELEUCID EMPIRES**
323			Ptolemy I
312	Ptolemy I takes Palestine		Seleucius king at Babylon
223			Antiochus III
203			Ptolemy V
198	Antiochus III takes Palestine		
175			Antiochus IV
167	Temple desecrated by Antiochus IV. Maccabean rebellion.		
164	Temple rededicated		
142	The Maccabean Kingdom		**ROMAN EMPIRE**
64			Pompey in Syria
63	Pompey takes Jerusalem		
53–43	Antipater, Procurator of Judea		
37	Herod the Great, King of Judea		
27			Augustus Caesar

(Dates are approximate)

Part of the Jordan Valley from Jericho

In spite of its small size Palestine has a very varied relief and climate. There are four main geographical regions:

1. *The Coastal Plain* – This includes the Plain of Acco, or Acre, to the north of Mount Carmel; the Plain of Sharon between Mount Carmel and Joppa; and the Plain of Philistia, south of Joppa.

2. *The Central Highlands* – These form the backbone of Palestine. The highlands of Galilee, however, are separated from the hill country of Samaria and Judea by the Plain of Esdraelon. The land where the Judean hills on the east descend steeply to the Jordan Valley is known as the Wilderness of Judea. On the west, between the hill country of Judea and the Plain of Philistia, lies the Shephelah, or Lowlands.

3. *The Jordan Valley* – This is part of a great rift valley which divides eastern and western Palestine. From its sources above Dan (329 metres above sea level) the river Jordan flows down to the Sea of Galilee (212 metres below sea level) and then to the Dead Sea (392 metres below sea level). The rift valley continues through the Arabah to the Red Sea and extends into East Africa.

4. *The Eastern Plateau* – This is divided by four rivers: the Yarmuk, Jabbok, Arnon and Zered. The height of the plateau, which is largely treeless but reasonably fertile, ranges from 600 to 1200 metres. The desert lies to the east.

Plain of Lebonah. The ancient frontier between Judea and Samaria ran along the foot of these hills

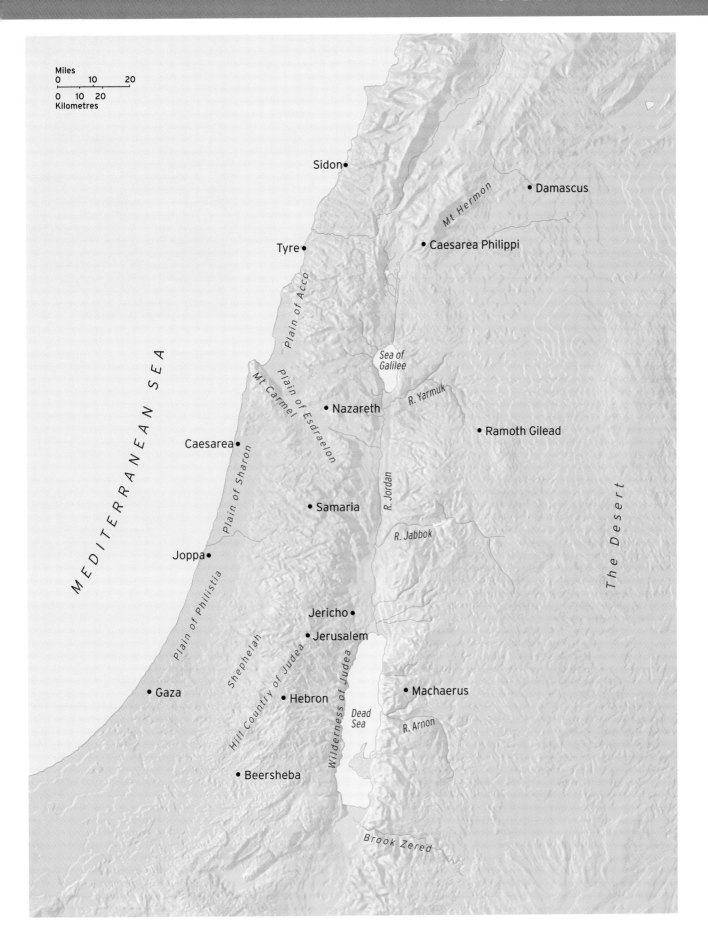

Miles
0   10   20
0 10 20
Kilometres

MEDITERRANEAN SEA

Sidon•

•Damascus

Mt Hermon

Tyre•

•Caesarea Philippi

Plain of Acco

Sea of
Galilee

Mt Carmel

Plain of Esdraelon

•Nazareth

R. Yarmuk

•Ramoth Gilead

Caesarea•

Plain of Sharon

R. Jordan

•Samaria

R. Jabbok

The Desert

Joppa•

Plain of Philistia

Jericho•

Shephelah

•Jerusalem

Hill Country of Judea

Wilderness of Judea

•Gaza

•Machaerus

•Hebron

Dead
Sea

R. Arnon

•Beersheba

Brook Zered

WHEN Jesus was born Palestine was part of the Roman Empire. But, as we have seen, it was governed by Herod the Great. When he died in 4 BC the land was divided into three main political areas which were governed by three of Herod's sons.

Archelaus ruled over Judea, Samaria and Idumea from 4 BC to AD 6 when the emperor Augustus placed them under the control of Roman procurators until AD 41. Their capital was at Caesarea, a coastal city built by Herod the Great. But during the Jewish festival of the Passover, the procurators stayed in Jerusalem at the Praetorium – the Roman headquarters where troops were stationed. This accounts for Pontius Pilate's presence in Jerusalem at the Passover when the Jews handed Jesus over to him (Mark 15).

Herod Antipas ruled over Galilee and Perea from 4 BC to AD 39. His first capital was at Sepphoris, four miles north of Nazareth, in Galilee. Later in his reign Antipas built a new capital on the western shore of the Sea of Galilee, which he named Tiberias in honour of the emperor. Jesus did not visit either of these non-Jewish cities. But He spent most of His life at Nazareth, and carried out much of His ministry in Galilee. This explains why Pilate sent Jesus to Herod Antipas during His trial (Luke 23:6–12). Antipas was also the King Herod who was responsible for beheading John the Baptist (Mark 6:14–30).

Philip ruled the area north-east of Galilee (Iturea and Traconitis) from 4 BC to AD 34. Like Herod Antipas, Philip also built a new city in honour of the emperor – Caesarea Philippi – which was his capital. Jesus visited this district before His transfiguration (Mark 8:27). He also visited another new city built by Philip: Bethsaida Julias, which is called Bethsaida in the Gospels (Mark 6:45; 8:22).

South of Philip's territory was the Decapolis – a Greek word meaning 'Ten Cities'. In this region there was originally a league of ten independent Greek cities which were protected by the Roman governor of Syria. The number of cities in the league, however, seems to have varied from time to time. Scythopolis, previously called Beth Shan, was the most important and the only one situated west of the Jordan. Among the others was Gerasa (known today as Jerash) and Philadelphia (now Amman, the capital of Jordan). During His ministry Jesus visited the Decapolis on at least two occasions (Matthew 8:28; Mark 7:31).

View of Bethlehem

Nazareth today

The Roman road from Jerusalem to Jericho

44

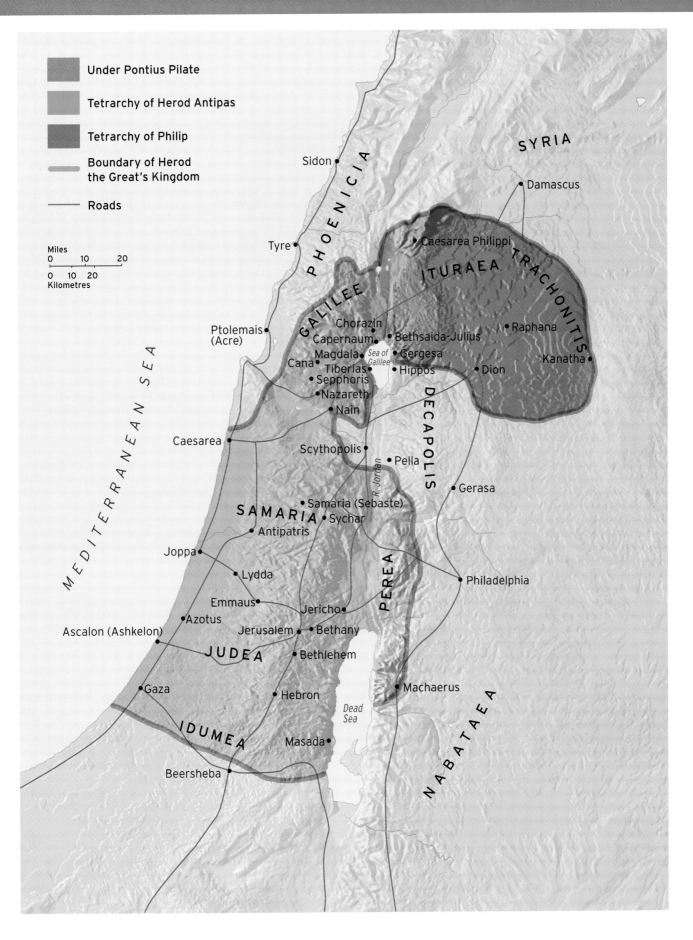

Under Pontius Pilate

Tetrarchy of Herod Antipas

Tetrarchy of Philip

Boundary of Herod
the Great's Kingdom

Roads

Miles
0   10   20
0   10   20
Kilometres

SYRIA

Sidon

Damascus

PHOENICIA

Tyre

Caesarea Philippi

ITURAEA

TRACHONITIS

GALILEE

Chorazin

Raphana

Capernaum

Bethsaida-Julius

Ptolemais
(Acre)

Magdala

Gergesa

Kanatha

Cana

Tiberias

Hippos

Sea of
Galilee

Sepphoris

Dion

Nazareth

DECAPOLIS

Nain

MEDITERRANEAN SEA

Caesarea

Scythopolis

Pella

R. Jordan

Gerasa

SAMARIA

Samaria (Sebaste)

Sychar

Antipatris

PEREA

Joppa

Philadelphia

Lydda

Emmaus

Jericho

Azotus

Jerusalem

Bethany

Ascalon (Ashkelon)

Bethlehem

JUDEA

Gaza

Hebron

Machaerus

Dead
Sea

NABATAEA

IDUMEA

Masada

Beersheba

JESUS spent much of His ministry – preaching, teaching and healing the sick – in the district of Galilee where most of the people of Palestine lived. The population was particularly large around the Sea of Galilee. Nine or ten towns surrounded the lake at that time and each had a population of no fewer than 15,000. Today only one remains – Tiberias. The sites of Magdala, Capernaum and Chorazin lie to the north of Tiberias, and those of Bethsaida, Gergesa and Hippos on the eastern side of the lake. But the sites of the other two or three lakeside towns are either uncertain or unknown.

Jesus made Capernaum the headquarters of His Galilean ministry (Matthew 4:12–13). As well as being a busy lakeside port Capernaum was also an important frontier town on the Via Maris, the Roman road from Egypt to Damascus. Peter and Andrew, James and John – the first disciples of Jesus – lived here (Mark 1:16–20), and so did Matthew, the tax-collector, another disciple (Matthew 9:9).

The River Jordan. Bethany beyond the Jordan is believed to be the site of Jesus' baptism

The Sea of Galilee

Church of the Beatitudes overlooking the Sea of Galilee

The Sea of Galilee, which was also called the Lake of Gennesaret and the Sea of Tiberias, is only 20 kilometres long and 11 kilometres across at its widest point. But in New Testament times it was famous for its fishing industry. Like some of the disciples, many of the people in the surrounding towns were fishermen. Others worked on the land, especially on the fertile Plain of Gennesaret, which was the market garden of Galilee.

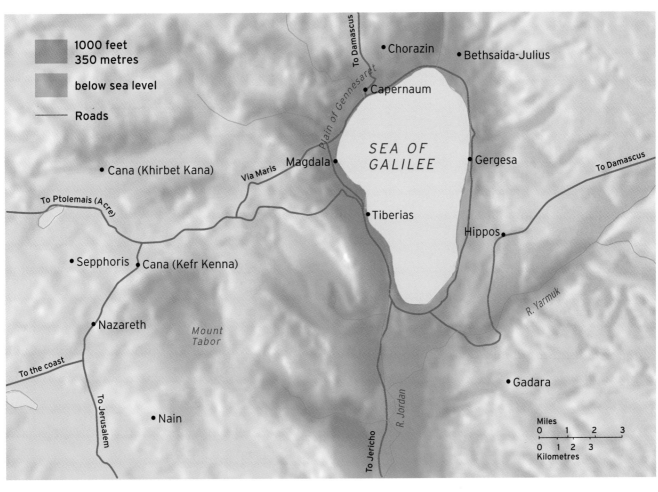

1000 feet
350 metres

below sea level

Roads

To Damascus

• Chorazin

• Bethsaida-Julius

Plain of Gennesaret

• Capernaum

Cana (Khirbet Kana)

Via Maris   Magdala •

SEA OF
GALILEE

• Gergesa

To Damascus

To Ptolemais (Acre)

• Tiberias

Hippos •

R. Yarmuk

• Sepphoris   • Cana (Kefr Kenna)

• Nazareth

Mount
Tabor

R. Jordan

To the coast

• Gadara

To Jerusalem

• Nain

To Jericho

Miles
0   1   2   3
0   1   2   3
Kilometres

Fishing boat
at Tiberias

The synagogue at
Capernaum

Mount Tabor – traditional site of the Transfiguration

The Garden of Gethsemane with the Golden Gate behind

AT THE time of Jesus, Herod the Great had transformed Jerusalem into a splendid city. The plan opposite shows the approximate position of Herod's walls, together with the sites which are known to have existed at that time. The exact course of Herod's northern wall is uncertain, but archaeological evidence indicates that the traditional site of the crucifixion – where the Church of the Holy Sepulchre now stands – lay outside the city walls at the time of Jesus. Today, however, it is situated inside the walls built by the Turks in the sixteenth century.

Jerusalem from the Mount of Olives

The Western, or Wailing, Wall of Herod's Temple

Church of the Holy Sepulchre – traditional site of the crucifixion

Archaeological excavations have also revealed a number of other sites in the city associated with Jesus. Among them is the Antonia Tower, a fortress built by Herod at the north-west corner of the Temple area. This is the traditional site of the Praetorium where Jesus was tried by Pontius Pilate (John 18:28–19:16). Excavated remains of the Pool of Bethesda, where Jesus healed a paralysed man (John 5:2–9), can also be seen. So too can the Pool of Siloam where Jesus healed a blind man (John 9:1–12). This pool was built by Hezekiah when he constructed his famous tunnel through the rock to channel the water from the Gihon Spring into the city (2 Kings 20:20).

Nothing remains of Herod's Temple, which was completely destroyed by Titus in AD 70. But the huge Temple area has been preserved, together with sections of its massive retaining walls – including the famous Western, or Wailing, Wall. Since the seventh century the Dome of the Rock, a Muslim shrine, has stood on the reputed site of the Temple's altar of burnt-offering.

The Garden Tomb.
Jesus was buried in a similar tomb

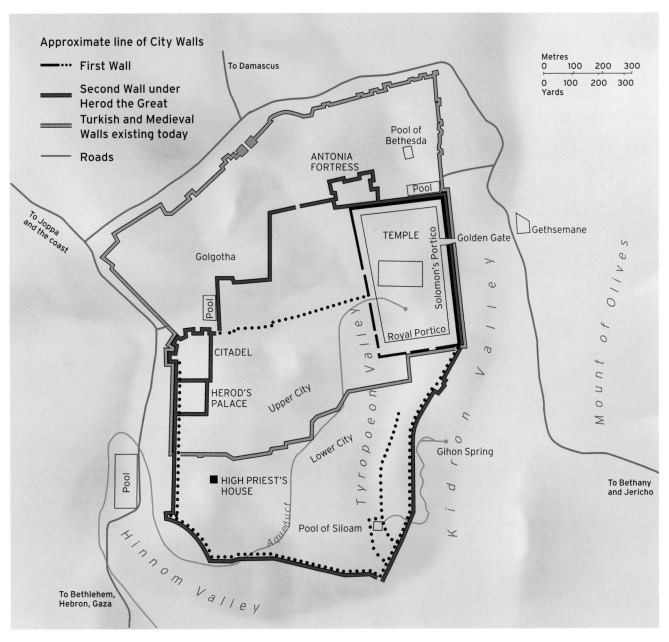

Approximate line of City Walls

- **First Wall**
- **Second Wall under Herod the Great**
- **Turkish and Medieval Walls existing today**
- **Roads**

To Damascus

Metres
0   100   200   300

0   100   200   300
Yards

Pool of Bethesda

ANTONIA FORTRESS

Pool

To Joppa and the coast

TEMPLE

Solomon's Portico

Golden Gate

Gethsemane

Golgotha

Pool

Royal Portico

Tyropoeon Valley

Mount of Olives

CITADEL

HEROD'S PALACE

Upper City

Lower City

Gihon Spring

Kidron Valley

To Bethany and Jericho

Pool

HIGH PRIEST'S HOUSE

Aqueduct

Pool of Siloam

To Bethlehem, Hebron, Gaza

Hinnom Valley

BEFORE His Ascension Jesus told His disciples to remain in Jerusalem until they received the gift of the Holy Spirit: '... you will receive power when the Holy Spirit comes on you' Jesus said, '... and you will be my witnesses in Jerusalem, and in all Judea and Samaria, and to the ends of the earth' (Acts 1:1–8).

Ten days after the Ascension, on the Jewish Festival of Pentecost, the disciples were filled with the Holy Spirit, as Jesus had promised (Acts 2:1–13). This important event marked the beginning of the Church's life and work, and the disciples immediately began to witness in Jerusalem to the resurrection of Jesus. Like Jesus, they were persecuted by the Jewish religious leaders, but thousands of Jews in Jerusalem were converted to the Christian faith as a result of their preaching and miracles.

After the martyrdom of Stephen, 'a great persecution broke out against the church at Jerusalem' (Acts 8:1). Apart from the apostles, who at first remained in Jerusalem, the persecuted Christians fled south to Judea, north to Samaria,

Phoenicia and Syria, and west to the coastal plain and Cyprus. But wherever they went the Christians told people about Jesus and made many converts.

Philip, for example, preached in Samaria, baptised an Ethiopian on the road to Gaza, and then preached in the towns of the coastal plain from Azotus to Caesarea (Acts 8:4–40). Later, the apostle Peter also visited the coastal plain, and made converts at Lydda, Joppa and Caesarea (Acts 9:32–43).

When Paul arrived in Damascus after his conversion, he found Christians there (Acts 9:1–9). At Antioch, the capital of Syria, a strong church of Jewish and Gentile converts had also been founded. Antioch soon became a very important Christian centre, and it was here that the disciples were first called Christians (Acts 11:26).

After sending Paul to Tarsus (Acts 9:30) the apostles sent him to Syrian Antioch in about AD 43 to teach the new converts the Christian faith (Acts 11:19–26). Five years later, about AD 47, Paul left Antioch on the first of his three missionary journeys (see pages 52–54). Meanwhile, by AD 45, there were Christians in Rome, the capital of the Roman Empire. According to tradition, the apostle Peter first preached the Christian faith in Rome, but the exact date of the church's foundation here is not known.

Roman Basilica, Samaria

St Peter's Cave Church at Antakya (Antioch), Turkey

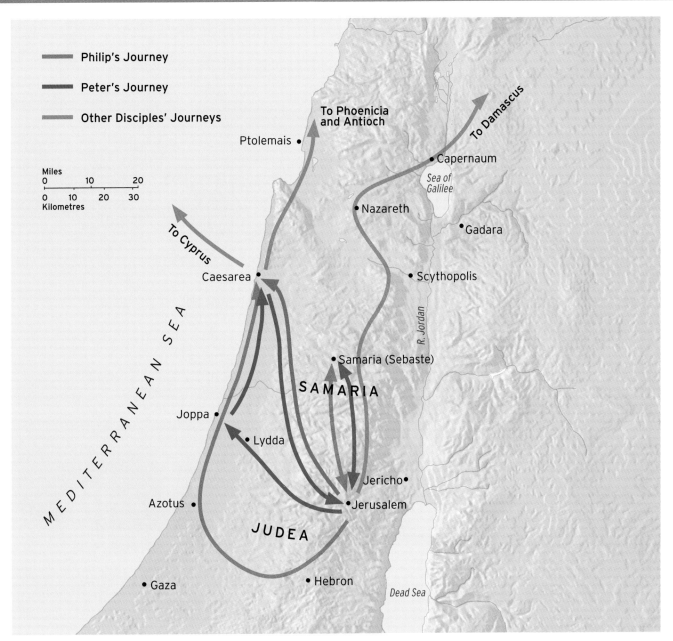

Philip's Journey

Peter's Journey

Other Disciples' Journeys

Miles
0   10   20
0 10 20 30
Kilometres

To Phoenicia and Antioch

To Damascus

Ptolemais

Capernaum

Sea of Galilee

To Cyprus

Nazareth

Gadara

Caesarea

Scythopolis

R. Jordan

MEDITERRANEAN SEA

Samaria (Sebaste)

SAMARIA

Joppa

Lydda

Jericho

Azotus

Jerusalem

JUDEA

Gaza

Hebron

Dead Sea

Roman habour at Caesarea

Philip's Fountain near Hebron

Simon's House, Joppa

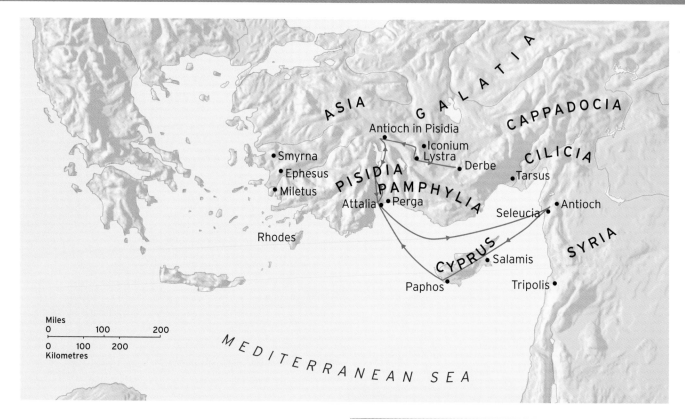

PAUL set out on his first missionary journey in the spring of AD 47, accompanied by Barnabas and John Mark (Acts 13 and 14). From Antioch in Syria they went to Seleucia, and sailed to Salamis in Cyprus. They crossed the island to Paphos where the Roman proconsul, Sergius Paulus, was converted. From Paphos the party sailed to Attalia (Antalya) in Asia Minor, and went on to Perga in Pamphylia. Here, perhaps because he was homesick, John Mark suddenly returned home to Jerusalem. But Paul and Barnabas continued their journey inland to Antioch of Pisidia, Iconium (Konya), Lystra and Derbe. They then retraced their steps to Attalia. From here they sailed back to Seleucia and returned to Antioch in the summer of AD 49. In spite of much opposition to their preaching Paul and Barnabas succeeded in making many converts, and Paul's Letter to the Galatians was probably written to the churches they founded in south Galatia.

Roman Gymnasium at Salamis, Cyprus

Perga gate at Antalya (Attalia), Turkey

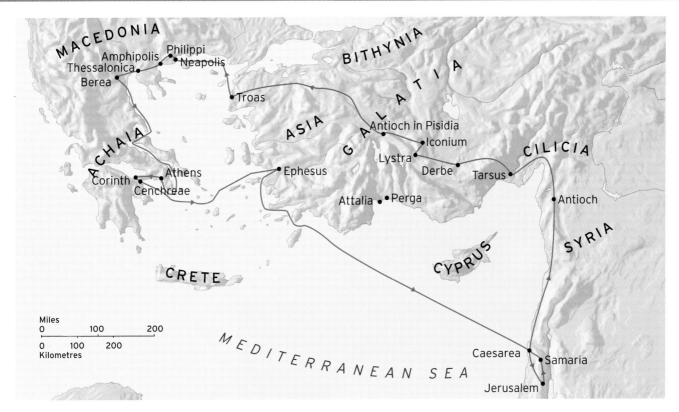

Main street of Roman Philippi, Greece

The Parthenon in Athens, Greece

PAUL left Antioch in Syria on his second missionary journey in the spring of AD 50 accompanied by Silas (Acts 15:36–18:22). From Antioch they travelled through Syria and Cilicia before visiting the churches Paul founded in south Galatia on his first journey. At Lystra they were joined by Timothy, a recent young convert.

In Galatia Paul, guided by the Holy Spirit, changed his proposed itinerary (Acts 16:6–7). Instead of preaching in Asia and Bithynia, the party travelled through Mysia to Troas where Luke, the author of Acts, joined them. From Troas they sailed to Neapolis (Kavalla) in Macedonia, and founded the first churches in Europe at Philippi, Thessalonica and Berea. Jewish opposition forced Paul to leave Berea and he went on to Athens and then to Corinth. After spending eighteen months in Corinth, Paul returned to Antioch in the summer of AD 53.

The theatre of
Ephesus, Turkey

Remains of Roman baths at Troas, Turkey

PAUL left Antioch on his last and longest missionary journey in the summer of AD 53 (Acts 18:23–21:16). This time he travelled by himself and, after visiting the churches in south Galatia, went to Ephesus where he stayed for over two years. During this time churches were founded not only in Ephesus but also in other parts of Asia. When a riot brought Paul's work at Ephesus to an end he went to Macedonia, and Achaia in Greece.

Paul was planning to sail from Greece to Syria when he heard of a Jewish plot to kill him. So instead he returned to Macedonia, and sailed from Neapolis. At Troas Paul was joined by delegates from various churches who accompanied him to Jerusalem with a collection for the poor Christians. They arrived in the summer of AD 57 and, as Paul expected, Jewish hostility soon led to his arrest and imprisonment.

THE Romans arrested Paul during a Jewish riot in Jerusalem and sent him to Caesarea, where he was imprisoned for two years from AD 57 to 59 (Acts 21:27–26:32). When Paul appealed to be tried by the emperor he was sent to Rome under escort by sea (Acts 27–28:16). In August AD 59 he sailed from Caesarea to Myra, in Lycia, where he boarded a ship bound for Italy. But south of Crete the ship was wrecked in a violent storm – without loss of life – off the island of Malta.

After spending three months in Malta, Paul continued his journey under escort by sea to Puteoli (Pozzuoli) in Italy. He then travelled overland to Rome where he arrived in February AD 60. Paul remained a prisoner in Rome for two years. Then, according to tradition, he was released and made further journeys before his final arrest and execution in Rome around AD 67.

Pyramid of Cestius in Rome, Italy

Statue of St Paul, Malta

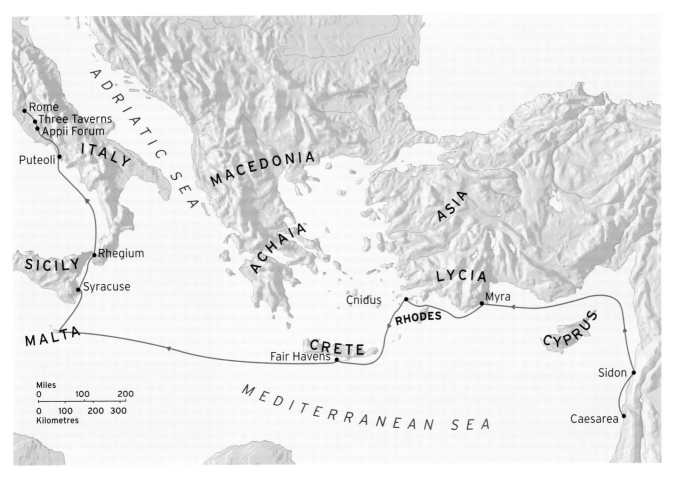

St John's Basilica at Ephesus, Turkey

Temple of Trajan in Pergamum, Turkey

THE spread of the Church to Asia Minor was mainly, but not entirely, due to the work of Paul. He certainly founded churches in south Galatia – at Antioch in Pisidia, Iconium, Lystra and Derbe – and probably in Pamphylia as well; for example at Perga (Acts 14:25). Paul was also the first to establish the Church in the Roman Province of Asia. But he was helped by Barnabas, Silas and Timothy who travelled with him in Asia Minor, and also by other Christian workers. Among those who helped him at Ephesus were Priscilla and Aquila (Acts 18:18), Gaius and Aristarchus (Acts 19:29) and Tychicus and Trophimus (Acts 20:4).

From Ephesus Paul also sent out workers to other cities in the Province of Asia where churches were established, for example, at Colossae, Hierapolis and Laodicea (Colossians 4:7–17). We know, too, that there were Christians at Troas and Miletus, and probably at Assos as well (Acts 20:5–17). From John's letters to the Seven Churches of Asia in the book of Revelation (Revelation 2 and 3) we learn that, towards the end of the first century AD, there were well-established churches at Smyrna, Pergamum, Thyatira, Sardis and Philadelphia, as well as at Ephesus and Laodicea.

However, other missionaries apart from Paul and his helpers were also founding churches in Asia Minor during the first century AD in areas which Paul did not visit: the First Letter of Peter is addressed to Christians in Pontus, Cappadocia and Bithynia, as well as Galatia and Asia (1 Peter 1:1). By the end of the first century AD, therefore, the Church had spread through most of Asia Minor, which later became an important area of Christianity in the East.

Remains of early Christian Basilica in Thyatira, Turkey

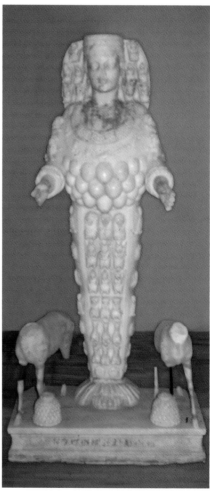

Statue of Diana at Ephesus, Turkey

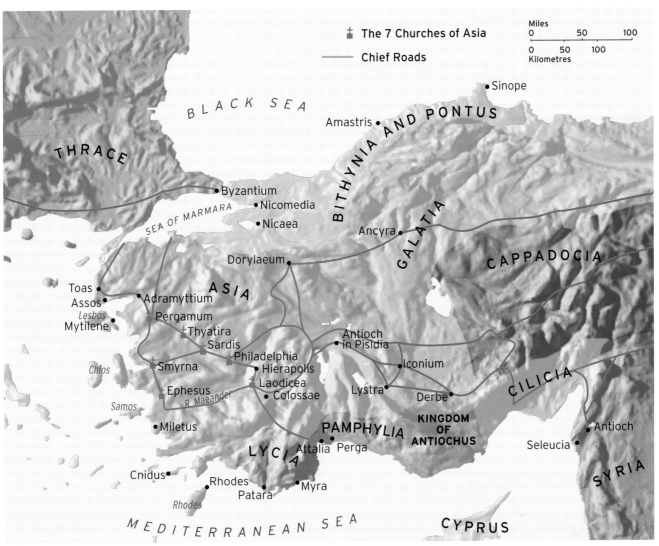

The 7 Churches of Asia
Chief Roads

Miles
0   50   100
0   50   100
Kilometres

BLACK SEA

THRACE

BITHYNIA AND PONTUS

• Sinope

Amastris •

• Byzantium
• Nicomedia
SEA OF MARMARA
• Nicaea

Ancyra •

GALATIA

CAPPADOCIA

Dorylaeum •

ASIA

Toas •
Assos •
Lesbos
Mytilene
• Adramyttium
Pergamum
✝ Thyatira
• Sardis
Chios
✝ Smyrna
Ephesus
R. Maeander
Samos
• Colossae
• Miletus

Philadelphia
• Hierapolis
Laodicea

Antioch
in Pisidia
• Iconium

Lystra •
• Derbe

KINGDOM
OF
ANTIOCHUS

CILICIA

• Antioch
Seleucia •

SYRIA

PAMPHYLIA

LYCIA
Attalia • Perga

Cnidus •
• Rhodes
Patara
• Myra
Rhodes

MEDITERRANEAN SEA

CYPRUS

Roman aqueduct at Smyrna (Izmir), Turkey

Temple of Artemis in Sardis, Turkey

Time Chart for the New Testament Period

BC	PALESTINE	NEW TESTAMENT EVENTS	THE ROMAN EMPIRE
6		Birth of Jesus	
4	Death of Herod the Great His kingdom divided between his sons: Archelaus ethnarch of Judea; Antipas tetrarch of Galilee and Perea; Philip tetrarch of Iturea and Traconitis		
AD			
6	Deposition of Archelaus and appointment of Roman Procurator		
14			Death of Augustus and accession of Tiberius
26	Pontius Pilate appointed	Beginning of Jesus' ministry	
29–30		Crucifixion, Resurrection and Ascension of Jesus Pentecost: the Church begins	
32–33		Martyrdom of Stephen and Conversion of Paul	
34	Death of Herod Philip		
35		Paul's first visit to Jerusalem	
36	Removal of Pontius Pilate		
37			Caligula
41	Herod Agrippa I King of Judea		Claudius
43		Paul in Antioch James the Apostle martyred	
44	Death of Herod Agrippa		
45–46		Paul's second visit to Jerusalem	
47–49		First missionary journey	
49		Third visit to Jerusalem for Council	
50–53		Second missionary journey	
50	Herod Agrippa II		
52	Felix appointed Procurator of Judea		
53		Paul's fourth visit to Jerusalem	
53–57		Third missionary journey	
54			Nero
57		Fifth visit to Jerusalem	
57–59		Paul's imprisonment in Caesarea	
59	Festus appointed Procurator	Paul appeals to Caesar Voyage to Rome	
60–62		Paul's imprisonment in Rome	
61		Death of James, the Lord's brother, in Jerusalem	
64	Florus the Procurator		Great fire in Rome; persecution of Christians
66	First Jewish Revolt		
67		Martyrdom of Peter and Paul	
68			Death of Nero
70	Jerusalem destroyed by Titus		
81–96		Persecution of Christians	Domitian
98			Trajan
100		Death of John the Apostle	
117			Hadrian
132	Second Jewish Revolt		
135	Jerusalem rebuilt by Hadrian and renamed Aelia Capitolina		
138			Death of Hadrian

(Dates are approximate)

Aqueduct pipes in Laodicea, Turkey

Remains of the city wall of Philadelphia, Turkey

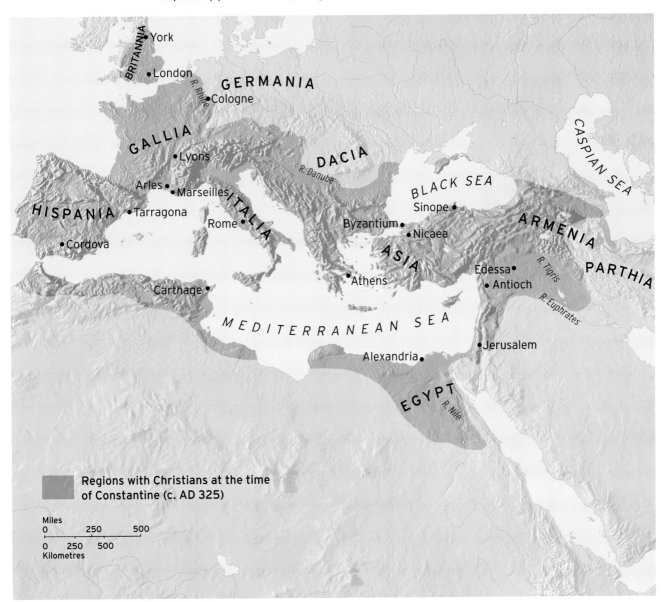

Regions with Christians at the time of Constantine (c. AD 325)

Miles
0   250   500

0   250   500
Kilometres

THE maps on pages 62–63 and 64 show only the most important archaeological sites in Bible lands, as since the nineteenth century numerous biblical and other ancient sites have been excavated, and new sites are continually being discovered and excavated.

In 1964, for example, Italian archaeologists who had been making a survey in north Syria decided to excavate a huge mound known as Tell Mardikh, 56 kilometres south of Aleppo. Nothing was known about the site. But, four years later, in 1968, an inscribed statue was unearthed which identified the site as Ebla. Little was

Jericho – defence tower dating from Neolithic times

known about this obscure ancient city. Then in 1975 archaeologists made a sensational discovery. In a room near the entrance to a royal palace that had been destroyed by fire around 2250 BC they found more than 15,000 clay tablets covered with cuneiform writing. They were the official state records of the kingdom of Ebla between approximately 2400 and 2250 BC.

Most of the tablets record details of Ebla's administration, commerce and foreign relationships. They reveal that, during the third millennium BC, Ebla was the capital of a previously unknown Middle Eastern empire and

civilisation. Among the other tablets are thirty-two bilingual dictionaries in Sumerian and Eblaite, a previously unknown west Semitic language. But most intriguing of all are the similarities between some of the tablets and parts of the Old Testament written more than a millennium later.

There are stories of the Creation and Flood, for example, similar to those in the book of Genesis. Also mentioned are names of cities in Palestine, such as Hazor, Megiddo and Jerusalem, which were thought to have been founded much later. So, too, are names known to us from Genesis such as Abraham, Ishmael and Esau. This has caused the biggest surprise amongst biblical scholars because the tablets were written four or five hundred years before the proposed dates of the Patriarchs. The excavations at Ebla, therefore, will not only open up a new chapter in the history of the Middle East, but also have a profound effect on biblical scholarship.

Excavations south-west of the Temple wall, Jerusalem

Ebla is but one example of the numerous archaeological sites which are adding to knowledge of the Bible and its historical background. Another is Ugarit (Ras-Shamra), an impressive site on the Mediterranean coast in north Syria, where excavations have been carried out for several decades. Among the many important discoveries made here were thousands of clay tablets from the libraries of two Canaanite temples dating from the fifteenth to fourteenth centuries BC. They were written in a previously unknown alphabetic script of thirty cuneiform signs, known as Ugaritic, which played an important part in the later development of writing. Some of the texts record stories about the Canaanite gods and goddesses such as El, Baal and Asherah. They have provided important new knowledge about the Canaanite religion, which had such a great influence on the Israelites. The high standard of Canaanite civilisation also had a great influence on the

Israelites as the excavations of Canaanite cities in Palestine have revealed, for example, at Gezer, Megiddo and Hazor.

Among the most important excavations in Palestine in recent times are those at Qumran where the first Dead Sea Scrolls were found in 1947. Others include the late Dame Kathleen Kenyon's excavations at Jericho in the 1950s and Jerusalem in the 1960s, which have completely altered our knowledge of the history and development of these sites. For example, she discovered that Jericho was occupied as early as approximately 9000 BC, and that the Jebusite city of Jerusalem, captured by David around 1000 BC, was situated on the steep eastern slopes of Mount Ophel.

Staircase to the Temple of Augustus, Samaria

Excavations at Ur which show evidence of the Flood

Excavations in progress near the Temple area, Jerusalem

Qumran Cave 4; site of the most significant find of Dead Sea Scrolls

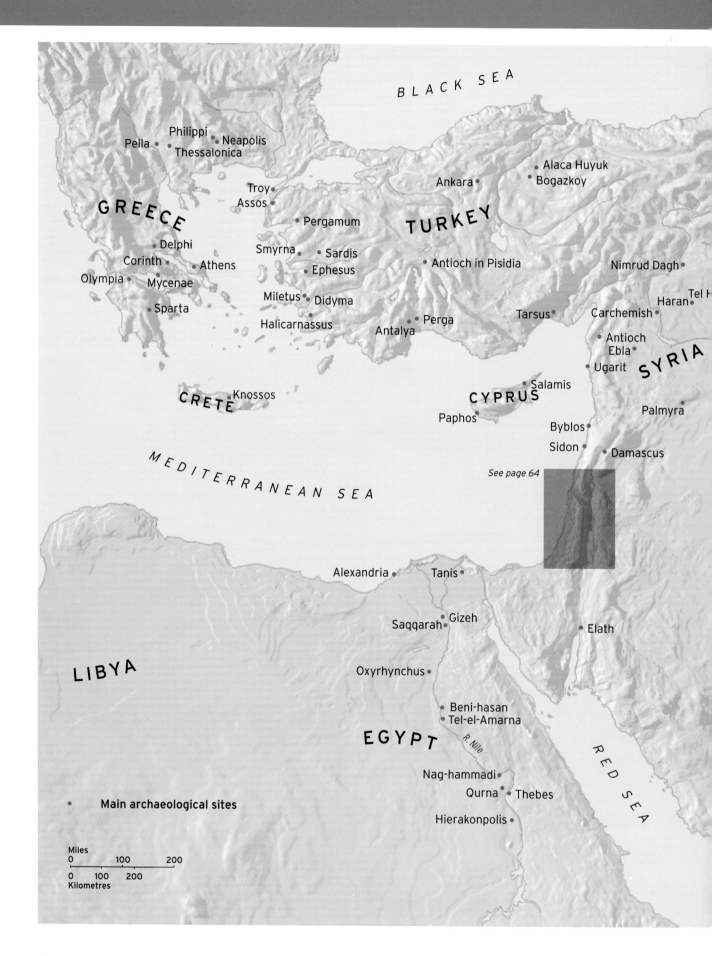

BLACK SEA

GREECE

Pella • Philippi
• Neapolis
Thessalonica

Troy •
Assos •

Delphi •
Corinth •
• Athens
Olympia • • Mycenae
• Sparta

Smyrna •
Pergamum •
• Sardis
• Ephesus

Miletus •
• Didyma
Halicarnassus

TURKEY

Ankara •

Alaca Huyuk •
• Bogazkoy

• Antioch in Pisidia

Nimrud Dagh •

Haran •
• Tel H

Carchemish •

Tarsus •

Antalya • • Perga

CRETE
• Knossos

MEDITERRANEAN SEA

CYPRUS
• Salamis

Paphos •

Antioch •
Ebla •
• Ugarit

SYRIA

Palmyra •

Byblos •
Sidon •
• Damascus

See page 64

Alexandria •
• Tanis

Saqqarah •
• Gizeh

Elath •

LIBYA

Oxyrhynchus •

Beni-hasan •
• Tel-el-Amarna

EGYPT

R. Nile

RED SEA

Nag-hammadi •
Qurna • • Thebes

Hierakonpolis •

• **Main archaeological sites**

Miles
0   100   200
0   100   200
Kilometres

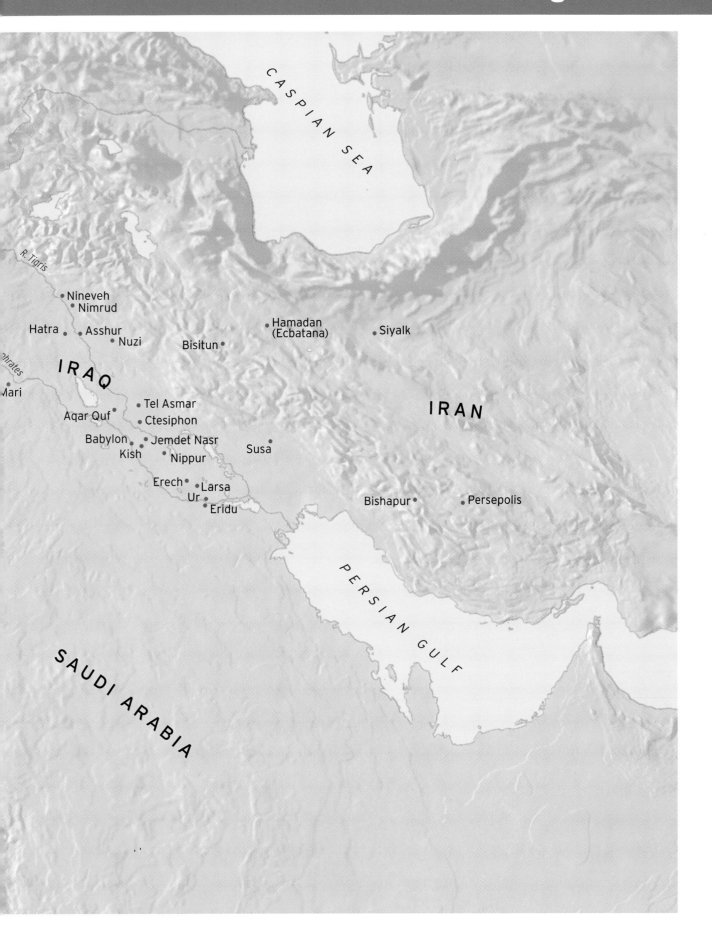

CASPIAN SEA

R. Tigris

Nineveh
Nimrud

Hamadan
(Ecbatana)

Siyalk

Hatra
Asshur
Nuzi

Bisitun

IRAQ

Euphrates

Mari

Tel Asmar

IRAN

Aqar Quf
Ctesiphon

Babylon
Jemdet Nasr
Kish
Nippur

Susa

Erech
Larsa
Ur
Eridu

Bishapur
Persepolis

PERSIAN GULF

SAUDI ARABIA

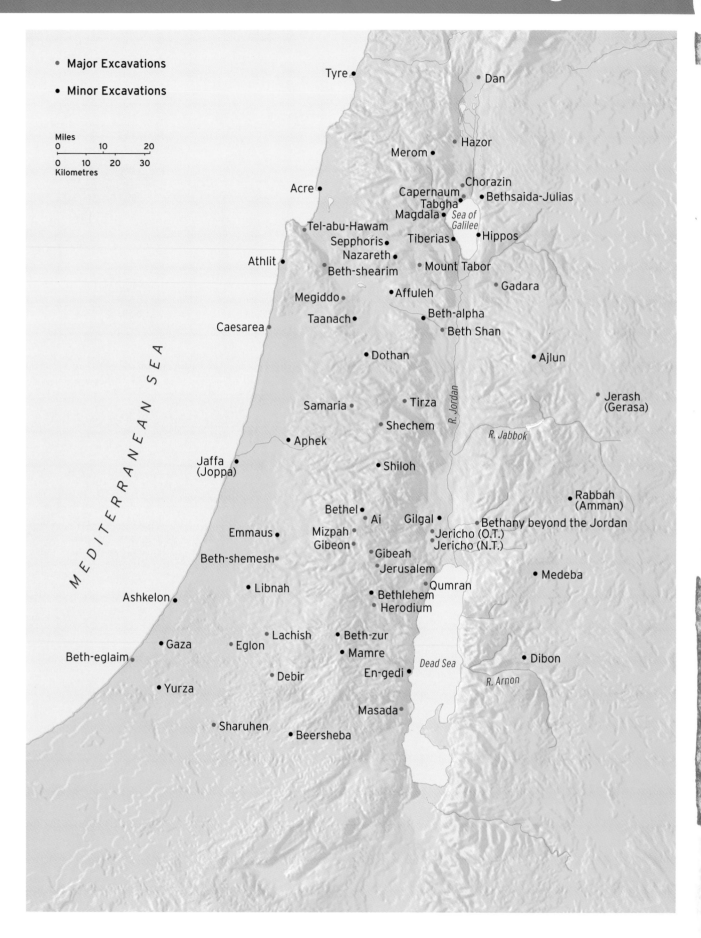

Major Excavations

Minor Excavations

Miles
0   10   20
0 10 20 30
Kilometres

Tyre

Dan

Hazor

Merom

Chorazin

Acre

Capernaum
Tabgha
Magdala

Bethsaida-Julias

Sea of
Galilee

Tel-abu-Hawam

Sepphoris

Tiberias

Hippos

Athlit

Nazareth

Beth-shearim

Mount Tabor

Gadara

Megiddo

Affuleh

Taanach

Beth-alpha

Caesarea

Beth Shan

MEDITERRANEAN SEA

Dothan

Ajlun

Samaria

Tirza

R. Jordan

Jerash
(Gerasa)

Shechem

R. Jabbok

Aphek

Jaffa
(Joppa)

Shiloh

Rabbah
(Amman)

Bethel

Ai

Gilgal

Bethany beyond the Jordan

Emmaus

Mizpah

Jericho (O.T.)

Gibeon

Jericho (N.T.)

Beth-shemesh

Gibeah

Jerusalem

Medeba

Libnah

Qumran

Ashkelon

Bethlehem

Herodium

Gaza

Lachish

Beth-zur

Eglon

Mamre

Beth-eglaim

Dibon

Debir

En-gedi

Dead Sea

R. Arnon

Yurza

Masada

Sharuhen

Beersheba

NICK JR

The BACKYARDIGANS™

This annual

belongs to

Ella-mame

Contents

EGMONT
We bring stories to life

First published in Great Britain 2008 by Egmont UK Limited
239 Kensington High Street, London W8 6SA
Created for Egmont by John Brown Publishing Group
Edited by William Petty • Designed by Sarah Edwards

ISBN 978 1 4052 3176 3
1 3 5 7 9 10 8 6 4 2
Printed in Italy

The Frozen North Race

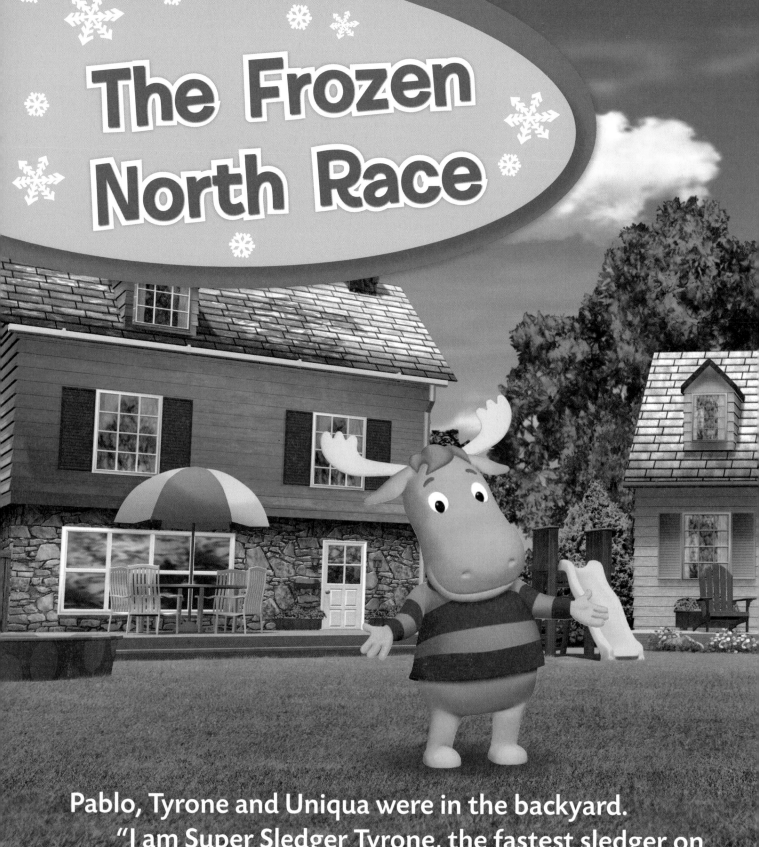

Pablo, Tyrone and Uniqua were in the backyard.
"I am Super Sledger Tyrone, the fastest sledger on the slopes!" said Tyrone. "I can outrace an avalanche!"
"Super Sledger Tyrone?" laughed Pablo. "More like Super SLUDGER!"

"You're no match for the super-speedy sledge of Speedster Pablo!" Pablo declared.

"Instead of arguing, put it to the test!" suggested Referee Uniqua. "Whoever wins the race is the fastest snow speeder in the Frozen North. Ready, get set, go!"

Let's get snow-going!

Speedster Pablo and Super Sledger Tyrone shot off downhill on their sledges. Soon, they came to a fork in the slope. Speedster Pablo skidded to the right, while Super Sledger Tyrone steered to the left. They both hoped they'd picked the quickest route to the finish.

Speedster Pablo met a hiker wearing earmuffs.

"You look cold!" said Hiker Tasha. "I've got a flask full of hot cocoa here. Would you like a cup?"

"Thanks, I'd love some!" said Speedster Pablo. "That will warm me up nicely, so I can keep speeding through this race."

Meanwhile, Super Sledger Tyrone had spotted an ice castle. But he came down the hill too fast, and got stuck in the snow.

Mountie on duty!

"You look like you could use some help, buddy!" said Austin the Mountie. "Let me dig you out."
"Thanks!" called Super Sledger Tyrone, as he shook off the snow and went on his way.

Speedster Pablo and Super Sledger Tyrone both
approached the finishing line. They hurtled downhill
at top speed, and crossed the finishing line ... at
exactly the same time!

   "You are both winners!" said Referee Uniqua.
"The prize goes to both of you!"

"Well, I guess I had a bit of help from Hiker Tasha," admitted Speedster Pablo.

"I suppose Austin the Mountie helped me," said Super Sledger Tyrone.

"Then the prize is for all of you," said Referee Uniqua. "Great teamwork!"

Everyone cheered. Then Uniqua had a good idea. "Who'd like bread and skis? I mean, cheese!" she said.

Winter Wonderland

Wrap up warm - and colour in this snowy picture!

How many snowflakes
are there in this
picture? Write the
number in the box!

13

17

Figure It Out!

Queen Tasha demands fruit! And she wants the same number of each kind. Which bowl should you bring her?

a

b   c

d   e

The villainous Dr Shrinky has been at work! Circle the two watering cans that are exactly the same size.

Draw lines to match the Backyardigans to their shadows. Which one doesn't have a shadow?

Space Race

Help Major Austin get home to Pablo! He can fly around the planets using his jetpack. But make sure he doesn't get lost in space!

START

FINISH

Mission to Mars

Look at these close-ups. Do you see where they come from in the big picture? When you find them, tick the boxes!

23

Spaceship Ride

Spaceman Pablo and Spacewoman Uniqua need a super-speedy new spaceship to travel into space! Finish off the spaceship below, and colour it in.

25

Dragon Ride

You have to be a really brave hero to ride a dragon!
These pictures look the same, but there are 10
differences in picture 2. Spot them all!

The Mighty Tower

Tasha and Uniqua were going to be explorers looking for adventure in the Deep Jungle.

"We will venture deep into the heart of the jungle, where no one has ever set foot before," said Explorer Tasha, excitedly.

Let's go on an adventure!

"Just because we've never been, doesn't mean no one has," pointed out Explorer Uniqua. "There are tribes that live in the jungle."

"Then we will go and find them!" said Explorer Tasha. "Let's get going!"

After travelling for many days, the brave explorers met a group of rather small people.

"Halt!" said one. "I am Chief Pablo. My tribe is small, but very strong. What is your business here?"

Watch out for jungle perils!

"We are brave explorers," said Explorer Uniqua.
"We wish to learn about your tribe."
Chief Pablo whispered to the other tribesmen for a
few minutes. Then he announced: "We have decided
to show you our Mighty Tower!"

"The Mighty Tower is what makes the people of our tribe so strong," explained Tribesman Austin, as they swung through the trees. "It gives us our power."

"It must be a really powerful tower!" whispered Explorer Uniqua to Explorer Tasha. "I bet it reaches high into the sky!"

"Yes, yes, it must have taken years to build," agreed Explorer Tasha.

But when they arrived, the explorers got a shock. The Mighty Tower was really ... a Mighty Flower! "We make tea from its leaves," explained the chief. "It tastes funny, but it makes us very strong. Perhaps you'd like a cup for your journey home?"

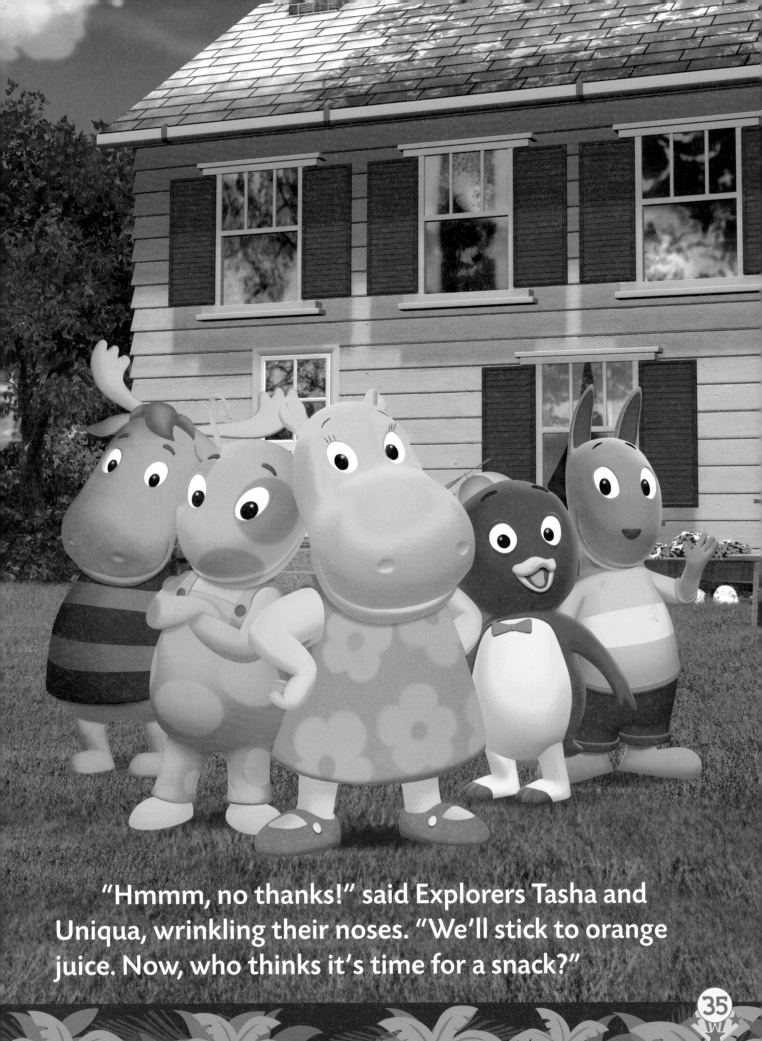

"Hmmm, no thanks!" said Explorers Tasha and Uniqua, wrinkling their noses. "We'll stick to orange juice. Now, who thinks it's time for a snack?"

Amazing Adventure

The Backyardigans are exploring a beach on a tropical island! Finish off the picture, and then colour it in.

Brain Teasers

Help Pablo surf to Tiki Beach by riding the waves in this order:

You can go up, down, left and right.

Only one of these is Tyrone's true reflection.
Draw a circle around the one you think it is.

a   b   c

Austin is a double
agent! Colour in each
section using the code
to reveal what every
super spy needs!

On the Road

a

b

c

d

e

Draw lines to match the shapes to the gaps in the picture. Which shape is left over?

1

2

MAP

5

4

3

6

Use this picture to help you!

Spy Games

Agent Secret needs to find Miss T in the streets of London, and get home! Watch out for broken-down buses blocking the streets.

START

How many buses are there in the picture? Count them!

FINISH

What's Wrong?

Look at this street scene. There are 7 things in it that are out of place. Tick the boxes as you find each one!

Pablo Sets Sail

Sailor wasn't much help today.

He dropped the as the sailed away.

Then spun the 's  too fast.

It came off in his hand and the sail fell off the mast!

 Pablo ship box blue

A rolled into the ocean .

The ship sprang a leak. Oh, what will Pablo do?

Now the ship is sinking and there's no more food.

Hungry Tyrone is now in a really bad mood!

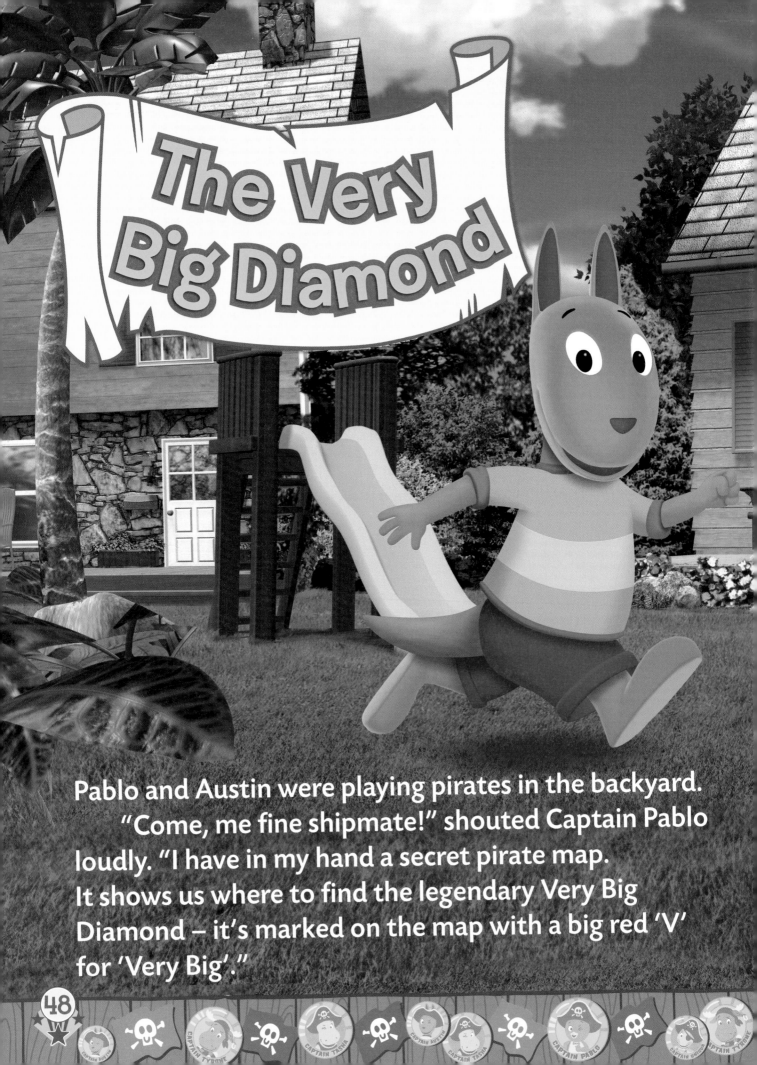

The Very Big Diamond

Pablo and Austin were playing pirates in the backyard. "Come, me fine shipmate!" shouted Captain Pablo loudly. "I have in my hand a secret pirate map. It shows us where to find the legendary Very Big Diamond – it's marked on the map with a big red 'V' for 'Very Big'."

But Captain Uniqua had the same idea. "Your map be hogwash!" she cried. "Only my map shows where the Very Big Diamond truly lies."

Pirates say ARRR!

"My map has an even bigger red 'V' for 'Very Big' on it," she added. They set off for opposite sides of the island with their maps, hoping to find the diamond.

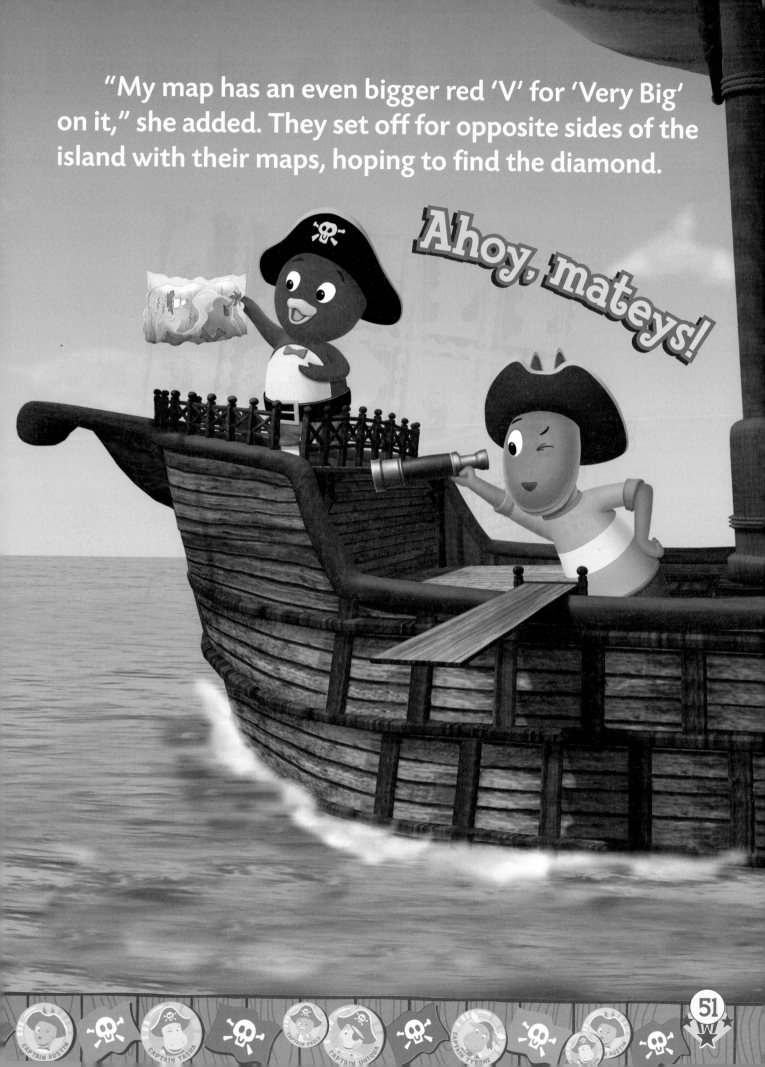

But when both crews had made their way across the island to the 'V' on their map, they got a surprise.
"What are ye doing here?" asked Captain Uniqua.
"This is where the 'V' is on OUR map!"

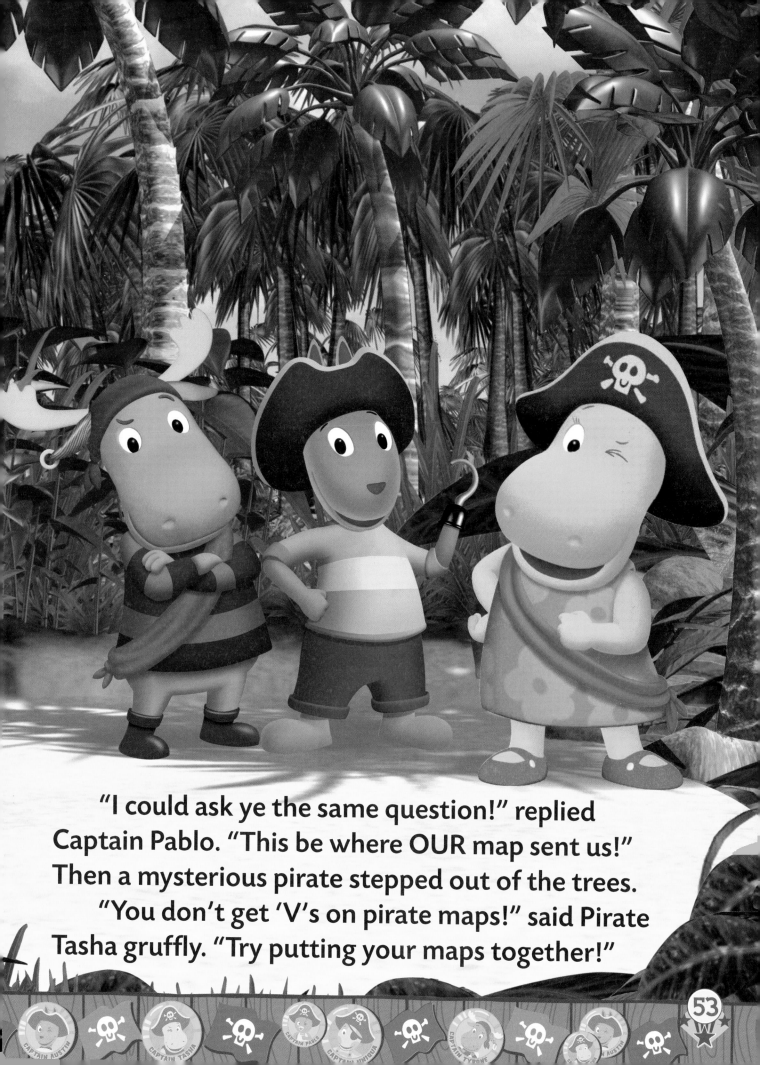

"I could ask ye the same question!" replied
Captain Pablo. "This be where OUR map sent us!"
Then a mysterious pirate stepped out of the trees.
"You don't get 'V's on pirate maps!" said Pirate
Tasha gruffly. "Try putting your maps together!"

It wasn't two 'V's – it was an 'X'! The pirates began to dig, and soon they had found a chest. Inside was something better than they'd expected – not a VERY Big Diamond, but an X-TREMELY Big Diamond!

"That diamond is big enough for all of us!" said Captain Uniqua. "Arrr you glad we worked together? Now let's keep searching! Has anyone got a map of the refrigerator?"

Shiver Me Timbers!

Join the dots to finish this pirate picture!
Then colour in the pirate pals.

1
2
20
3
4
19
18
17

57

Rope 'Em!

Yee ha! Cowboy Pablo has some horses to round up. Find a route that takes him back to the ranch, passing all the white horses, but none of the brown horses.

START

How many horses are there altogether? Write the number in the box.

FINISH

Cowboy Colouring

Howdy, partners! Grab some crayons, and have yourself a colouring-in hoedown!

61

Spooky Old House

Look at these close-ups. Do you see where they come from in the big picture? Circle them when you find them.

Backyard Puzzles

Look at the picture of Pablo, Uniqua and Tyrone hurdling, then answer the following questions:

Who has jumped the most hurdles?

Who has the most still to go?

64

Which shadow exactly matches Cowgirl Uniqua?

a   b

c   d

Circle the 2 juggling balls that are exactly the same.

How many juggling balls are there altogether?

Go For Goal!

Use the code to colour in these star players!

Goodbye!

Everyone's a winner!
Colour in this picture,
and wave goodbye.

68

Answers

Page 16 There are 13 snowflakes.

Page 18 Bowl c has equal amounts of fruit.

Page 19 1d, 2b, 4c, 5a. 3 has no shadow.

Page 20

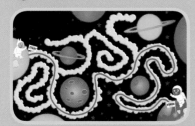

Page 22

Page 26

Page 38

Page 39 b is the matching reflection.

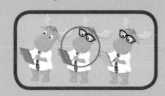

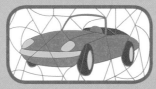

Page 40 1a, 2c, 3d, 4e, 6b. Shape 5, the rectangle, is left over.

Page 42 There are 15 buses.

Page 44

Page 58 There are 10 horses.

Page 62

Page 64 Pablo has jumped the most hurdles (3). Uniqua has the most hurdles still to jump (2).

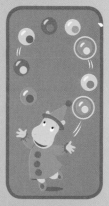

Page 65 There are 8 juggling balls in all.

69